Juggle

chief juggler®

D0369418

Ian Sanders is an entrepreneur, project manager, ideas-producer, marketing consultant and writer who has been juggling for 20 years. In 2008 Ian was included in the Business category of the *Courvoisier The Future 500*, a network of Britain's 'rising stars'. His career has embraced event production, broadcasting, broadcast services and marketing working with brands including MTV, Benetton, *The Financial Times* and Pepsi.

Since 2005 Ian has been running OHM, a marketing and business consultancy that helps clients exploit their market potential. Here he juggles a portfolio that extends from big projects for global clients through to one-off assignments for one-person start ups. In all he does, Ian trades on 'making a difference'.

Ian's first book *Leap! Ditch Your Job, Start Your Own Business & Set Yourself Free* was published by Capstone in January 2008.

He lives in Leigh-on-Sea with his wife and two sons. Find out more about Ian at www.iansanders.com and visit his blog at www.planetjuggle.com.

Author photo by Steven Mayatt.

Juggle!

Rethink Work, Reclaim your life

Ian Sanders

CAPSTONE

John Wiley & Sons Ltd, The Atrium, Southern Gate, Chichester,
West Sussex PO19 8SQ, England
Telephone (+44) 1243 779777

Email (for orders and customer service enquiries): cs-books@wiley.co.uk
Visit our Home Page on www.wiley.com

Other Wiley Editorial Offices

John Wiley & Sons Inc., 111 River Street, Hoboken, NJ 07030, USA

Jossey-Bass, 989 Market Street, San Francisco, CA 94103-1741, USA

Wiley-VCH Verlag GmbH, Boschstr. 12, D-69469 Weinheim, Germany

John Wiley & Sons Australia Ltd, 42 McDougall Street, Milton, Queensland 4064, Australia

John Wiley & Sons (Asia) Pte Ltd, 2 Clementi Loop #02-01, Jin Xing Distripark, Singapore 129809

John Wiley & Sons Canada Ltd, 6045 Freemont Blvd. Mississauga, Ontario, L5R 4J3 Canada

Wiley also publishes its books in a variety of electronic formats. Some content that appears in print may not be available in electronic books.

Library of Congress Cataloging-in-Publication Data

Sanders, Ian, 1968-
  Juggle! : re-think work, re-claim your life / by Ian Sande.
    p. cm.
  Includes index.
  ISBN 978-1-906465-37-7 (pbk. : alk. paper)   1. Career development.
2. Self-realization.   3. Quality of work life. I. Title.
  HF5549.5.C35S26 2009
  650.1–dc22

                                                          2008047081

British Library Cataloguing in Publication Data

A catalogue record for this book is available from the British Library
9781906465377
ISBN 978-1-90646537-7 (PB)

Typeset in 12 on 15 pt Baskerville MT by SNP Best-set Typesetter Ltd., Hong Kong
Printed and bound in the United Kingdom by TJ International Ltd.

For Zoë, Barney and Dylan
Thanks for putting up with me
through all my juggling

Contents

Preface   x
Acknowledgements   xiv
Meet the Jugglers   xv
Introduction   1

Part One: RETHINK WORK: BUST SOME MYTHS

1 'Change is bad'   7
2 'Success is about doing one thing'   8
3 'Specialism wins'   11
4 'Generalisation is bland'   13
5 'If you want to be good in business, consult the
   rule book first'   16
6 'Work is done in an office'   18
7 'Productivity = hours worked'   21
8 'It's all about the money'   24
9 'A job is for life'   25
10 'Your job title counts'   27
11 'Keep family out of it!'   29
12 'In search of the eternal work/life balance'   32
13 'You have to stick with the status quo'   34

Part Two: REDESIGN YOUR LIFE: THINK 'JUGGLE'!

1 Set your personal Sat Nav   39
2 Become your very own architect   42
3 Enjoy living a blur   44
4 Corporate juggling   46

5	Celebrate your multi-dimensional talents	48
6	Be the real you	51
7	Playing it your way	53
8	Think constant re-invention	55
9	Being adept at gear shifting	57
10	The importance of playtime	59
11	Being authentic	61
12	Learning on the job	63
13	Staying hands-on	65
14	Be an 'accidental success' – the importance of the non-plan!	66
15	The truth about multi-tasking	69

Part Three: HOW TO DO IT ALL: JUGGLE TACTICS

1	Manage time, all the time, every time	73
2	Segment your juggling	76
3	Be a listophile	78
4	Make it a project	80
5	Prioritise	81
6	Focus, focus, focus	84
7	Get unplugged	86
8	Bust your stress	88
9	Getting connected	91
10	Build effective relationships	93
11	Ask yourself (often): 'where is the value in what you are doing *right now*?'	96
12	Sell yourself!	99
13	Be a one-man brand	101
14	Expect the unexpected	103
15	Immerse yourself	105
16	Be prepared to press delete	106
17	Dealing with those damn meetings	108
18	Filter the crap!	110
19	What's your script?	111
20	Managing your identity	114
21	What to do with your quirky side?	116
22	Create your juggle jungle!	119
23	Having places to do and be	121
24	Go on an inspiration jaunt	123

25	Give yourself a treat and the importance of 660 seconds	126
26	Don't be a workaholic	128
27	Remember to come up for air	131
28	Be fit to juggle!	133
29	What turns you on?	135
30	Having a team	137
31	Delegate and outsource	138
32	Hire a digital assistant	141
33	Lose the guilt!	143
34	Sorting out the home life	144
35	Set the alarm clock!	146
36	Think: what's next?	148

Part Four: HOW TO HAVE IT ALL: JUGGLE LIFESTYLE

1	Look at success differently	154
2	What you do for love and what you do for money	157
3	Create a sustainable economic model and a sustainable lifestyle model	160
4	Jugglers have just got to have fun	163
5	You don't need to be the boss to have it all	166
6	Living life version 3.4	168
7	Having freedom of choice	170
8	Retire retirement	172
9	The work you = the real you	174
10	Are you a lifeaholic?	177
11	Ticking your boxes	178
12	Have you worked out what's *really* important?	181
13	Live in the now and fulfil your dreams	183
14	The bottom line = leave a legacy	186
15	It's make your mind up time	187
	The juggler's manifesto	190
	Index	193

PREFACE

I've been a Juggler all my working life. I've never mastered the art of actually juggling balls in the air, but from the age of 17 when I mixed school studies, a Saturday job and working in a radio station, right through my career, I've always striven to follow my heart and do more than one thing.

Some parts of that last 20 years' career stand out more than others. Interviewing Billy Bragg when I was 17, guarding Prince Charles by standing between him and a lighting tripod, interviewing Christian Slater, making tea for Sister Sledge, shaking hands with Tony Blair and Stevie Wonder (not at the same time), being an escort to *Mr Blobby*,* working backstage at The MTV Europe Music Awards. From photocopying scripts to attending board meetings I've done a lot. And I love that diversity.

That 'bunch of weirdness' is who I am, the anathema of a carefully crafted career plan. It's not just been about earning a living, but having fun and living my dreams. That's in contrast to the career routes that our parents' generation took.

Mr Blobby was a character from a primetime BBC TV show 'Noel's House Party'.
He was pink and yellow and I spent a lot of time with him in 1993 (long story) …

In my last proper job I carved out a unique role as corporate Juggler with a 'make it up as you go along' portfolio. I was managing director of one division, set up an operation at a new site, organised the company away day, managed joint venture projects, and edited the company newsletter. All at the same time. Going self-employed enabled me to re-invent myself free of a single job title, instead defined by a handful. But proof that whether you work for a big corporation, a small business or are self employed, you can still choose to be a Juggler.

I still find it difficult describing to others what I do; summing that up in a one-word description. I've just always done 'stuff' (media, marketing, events, projects). These two snapshots sum up the enigma of my recent life as a Juggler:

***Juggle Moment* #1 – October 2003.** A Thursday night in the basement of a pub in Islington, London N1 and I am crouching on the floor trying to stop a crazy bunch of enthusiastic Japanese fans from diving on to the tiny stage. On stage: Brigade, an Anglo-Japanese rock band. It's one of my latest business ventures: advisor to Open Top Music, Brigade's management company. Talk about hands-on management! The venue is dripping with sweat as I push the small crowd back. This is one of Brigade's first gigs and the crowd is loving it. I take a sip at my beer and smile at the juxtaposition between this and my other projects. I'm doing this one minute; managing an ad campaign for a big company the next, mixing bands with brands. Working on the band project was not about the money but it was new, it was different, it was fun. And most importantly – it was ME. Working with my business partners in uncharted territory, trying to get a new band established. An example of what you can do in this *scrambled up world of work*; with no rules, no limits, no 'can't do' list, but a passion to enjoy whatever you do.

***Juggle Moment #2* – May 2005.** I am sipping another drink on board *Octopus*, then the world's biggest private yacht, moored offshore at the Cannes Film Festival. I'm at a party hosted by Microsoft co-founder Paul Allen, who also happens to be the 7th richest man in the world. Guests include the film director George Lucas and the designer John Rocha (people known for their singular exceptional talent) and some bloke called Ian Sanders who we're not sure exactly what he does. Guests mingle and talk is of what business we're doing at the festival. I consider answering 'a bit of this and that' before confessing the truth, 'I just came for the party.' I take it all in as I look back at the shore line and feel it's a long journey from the A13 – the main road out of where I grew up in Essex – to Le Croisette. I'm reminded of what my friend and former colleague Emily had recently emailed me:

> *"It is great how much you seem to be achieving without actually (still) doing any actual concrete work."*

And she had a point. How *did* I get away with all this: living the life of a Juggler, carving out a unique work life, making it up as I go along?

I'm not quite sure how I got here. I guess it was by accident; definitely not a grand plan. If anything, it was based on an all-embracing philosophy to do 'Everything I Fancied'.

I soon realised I was not the only one juggling. Friends and clients were doing it. People I met, people I read about. Whether they are working for employers or doing their own thing, what unites such people is not just a desire to succeed, but to carve out their own work life mixed up with their personal passions. The intention – of course – is to keep all the balls in the air.

~ ~ ~

To kick off writing this book, I took an 'inspiration jaunt' to France. I needed a similar trip to help finish it, so I went to Amsterdam. In between those Destination Book-Ends it was bloody hard work. Juggling the book with my consultancy business, with clients, projects, a holiday, weekends, my wife and two sons. That journey was tough but it gave me a real life case study in juggling.

This is my Juggle Story.

Ian Sanders, Amsterdam, August 2008

Blog and video interviews with jugglers at www.planet juggle.com and more propaganda at www.iansanders. com

ACKNOWLEDGEMENTS

A round of applause to the Jugglers: Kevin Roberts, Roxanne Darling, Gary Vaynerchuk, Melanie Greene, Mike Southon.

Thanks to the other jugglers I have spoken to: David Sloly, Cheryl Goldenberg, Chris White, Mark Rowles, Richard René, Andy Bird, Dave Shields, Jan Simon, Trevor Campbell, Sam Bompas, David Prior and Ian Burrell.

Thanks go to Steven Mayatt, Matt Sitomen, Peter Morris, Ricky Burgess, Paul Ingle and Emily Morris for helping with Project Juggle. To Sarah, Jenny, Iain, Megan and Grace at Capstone for helping turn this idea into reality.

To Zoë and the boys.

Thanks to London, Leigh-on-Sea, Nice, Cornwall, Amsterdam and Paris, fuelled on fresh air and far too many espressos. …

MEET THE JUGGLERS

I've been lucky enough to meet and work with some fascinating people over the years. Some of their stories are contained here in *Juggle!*

I have also assembled a panel of five Jugglers who are at the pinnacle of their respective fields and who have been kind enough to share their experiences.

Let's meet the Jugglers:*

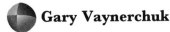 **Gary Vaynerchuk**

Gary is co-owner and Director of Operations at Wine Library, a $50m wine retail business. He presents *Wine Library TV*, a daily wine-tasting video blog that has made him into an Internet celebrity with various appearances on US television. He's the author of the bestselling book *101 Wines*. More recently, Gary has become known for his talents outside the wine world as a commentator on entrepreneurship, Web 2.0, social networking and personal branding. He is based in New Jersey, USA.

www.garyvaynerchuk.com
www.winelibrary.tv

---

* Some people have suggested this panel is a bit US-biased for a UK author. As it happens, Kevin and Melanie are both Brits, they just happen to be doing their thing based in the States (OK, Kevin is British born, now a NZ citizen).

 **Kevin Roberts**

Kevin is the New York-based CEO Worldwide of Saatchi
& Saatchi – one of the world's leading creative organisations with a team of over 7000 people across 83 countries.
Kevin is also the inaugural CEO in Residence at Cambridge University's Judge Business School, Chairman of
USA Rugby, a Director of New Zealand Telecom, a
trustee of the Turn Your Life Around Trust and a Sponsor
Governor of Lancaster Royal Grammar School. He is the
author of *Lovemarks* and *The Lovemarks Effect*. Now a New
Zealand citizen, he has offices and homes in Auckland
and New York, and homes also in St Tropez and Grasmere in the English Lake District.
www.krconnect.blogspot.com
www.saatchikevin.com

 **Melanie Greene**

Melanie is a Hollywood manager, producer and
founder of an eponymous talent firm whose clients
include David Duchovny and Michael Sheen. She
recently took on a partner and became co-founder of
Affirmative Entertainment and Productions – her
expanded client roster now also includes Oscar winners
Jennifer Connelly, Cher and Richard Dreyfus. She is
credited with turning a string of British TV actors such
as Lucy Davis into Hollywood stars. Melanie is Co-
Executive Producer of the hit TV show *Californication*

and has also produced and executive produced a number of other films and television series. *The Independent* newspaper recently named Melanie as one of the top twenty Brits in the US entertainment industry. She is based in Los Angeles.

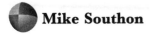 **Mike Southon**

Mike is one of the UK's top business speakers and a leading authority on entrepreneurship and sales, delivering over 100 presentations every year, all over the world. Mike also has a weekly column – 'My Business' in the weekend *Financial Times*, and a weekly podcast interview with leading entrepreneurs and business people. He is an experienced entrepreneur and founder of the Beermat Entrepreneur business network. He has co-authored several bestselling books, including *The Beermat Entrepreneur*. When he's not speaking for some of the world's leading companies, he performs on stage as his alter ego, 'Mike Fab-Gere', fronting a 60s/70s cover band. Mike is based in London.

www.beermat.biz

www.ft.com/comment/columnists/mikesouthon

 **Roxanne Darling**

Roxanne is the Hawaii-based coach, new media advisor, video blogger, and speaker. Her daily video blog *Beach Walks TV*, where she gives advice and inspiration on a range of personal and business issues, has brought her an international audience. Roxanne is co-owner of Bare Feet Studios where she advises clients on social media internet branding.

www.beachwalks.tv
www.barefeetstudios.com

But you don't have to be at the peak of your career or a business guru to be a successful Juggler. Throughout the book are tales and experiences of a broad range of people from the grassroots to the boardroom, all proving what is possible when you juggle.

This is for all existing and wannabe Jugglers, everywhere.

INTRODUCTION

We are all obsessed by it.
That 4-letter word.
We spend our lives doing it, thinking about it, talking about it.

WORK.

So if you're not doing it right or you don't like it, then you have a problem.

It's time to rethink Work, and re-frame it so it's more an extension of our personality. It's time to bust a few myths about what you should and shouldn't do.

We need to make choices in our life of what we want and how we do it. And if you don't like it, you change it. You can re-invent yourself and carve out a new work life.

You can choose to become a Juggler, to throw the rules out of the window, to create a life where you mix stuff you do for love and stuff you do for money. A life where you re-define success not by a salary package alone but by freedom, enjoyment, flexibility and lifestyle. Where work is an extension of You, reflecting your personality, your talents and desires; where you juggle different projects to be stimulated as well as to earn a living.

And the bottom line is, there is an option out there where you can strive to do your own thing and have it all.

Juggle! **is not about outsourcing your life, or how to sit with your feet up for the rest of your life. It's not about doing less – if anything, it's about doing more – it's about making work** *work* **for you.**

~ ~ ~

WE'VE ALL GONE PLURAL

When I took the leap to go it alone back in 2000, one of my mentors congratulated me and said, 'Well done, you've gone plural.'

And he was right: plurality of ideas, clients, disciplines and business activities is what going it alone is all about. Now everyone seems to have gone plural: mixing work and play, business and families, roles and projects; executives carving out roles where multiple projects and responsibilities vie for attention.

Increasingly we are ideas-rich yet time-poor. Our lives are full of growing to-do lists, jobs to do, ideas to develop but not enough hours in the day. We don't want to be slaves to our bosses or our *BlackBerries*; we want to be in control of our destiny.

How the heck do you juggle all this? How do you ensure that you can deal with the increasing demands on your time? And more crucially, how can you create a role for yourself that reflects the real you and gives you greater success? A re-invented professional identity that enables you to have the best of both worlds, to mix up work and play? This is the essence of *Juggle!*

Plurality of disciplines and hats is not just good for your health; it also can be good for your wealth. We live in a radically changing world with tough trading conditions and survival is about flexibility and resilience. Sticking to one business model to one product, to one market is limiting. You have to embrace plurality.

And if you PUT more in, you can get more OUT.

David Sloly is Creative Director at the UK digital marketing agency Mason Zimbler; he's a great advocate of mixing things up. Here's David's take on it – this is Real Life, 2008:

'It's like my whole work life is an algorithm pushing and pulling agendas up and down the priority list. I'm no longer a worker, I'm an editor, making real time decisions as to what must be done right now, next, tomorrow. Play and work are the same. I play, clear my head, come up with a solution for a client's problem, go to work on it, feel tired, go and play to relax. This lifestyle, if edited correctly, can only be described as damn beautiful.'

This book is for every one of you who wants to live a fulfilling and authentic life made up of your passions and desires. You'll need three essential ingredients to be a successful Juggler: **Courage**, **Confidence** and **Talent**.

I will give you tips on how to juggle more effectively and show you how to redesign your work life with ideas and stories from other Jugglers along the way.

Juggle! is about embracing a mindset: it's a new way of thinking, but also a new way of doing. It's not about quitting the 9–5, but rather re-framing your relationship with work. It's not about putting your dreams and passions on hold, but integrating them now.

And the good news is, if you get your juggling right, it can improve your life, business and career.

Part One

RETHINK WORK: BUST SOME MYTHS!

In the late 1980s as a teenager, I remember anticipating my working life with some trepidation. I loved music and going to gigs but was worried that entering the world of work would mean I'd have to wear a suit, become all serious and leave all that behind. Thank goodness it was not like that; work is changing and it's not about going to a flash office in a flash suit any more. And you don't have to leave your personality at the door.

But lots of myths still prevail when it comes to work and business. Myths about how you should work, how productivity is measured and how you develop your career.

It's time to knock them down, to challenge some assumptions and change your thinking. Business success is not about specialism, it's actually about juggling a number of talents. And forget Work/Life Balance, it's more Work/Play Integration, it's about mixing 'It' all up.

Rethink 'Work', broaden your horizons and be thankful for your multi-dimensional talents. Our DNA is multi-faceted, it's plural, not singular – we are all unique, and our work life can reflect that. And in this age of abundance, workers have to be more multi-faceted to stand out and survive.

It's about a life where we juggle stuff.
Juggling hats, roles and balls.
Stuff we do for money and stuff we do for love.
Work. Family. Hobbies.

And that gives us some challenges but also some fantastic opportunities along the way.

'Given the virtual world that we live in and the liberation of mobility and interactivity provided by WiFi, email, mobiles, and iPods, there is no excuse for leaving anything on the table. By re-thinking the old, traditional norms (both at work and in terms of family) you can live a much more rewarding and full life. Work delivers achievement and fulfilment, and is an integral part of what I do.'

Kevin Roberts

Myth 1

'Change is bad'

For every one of us, the work and business landscape is changing. We have no idea where it's going. I have – literally – no idea what precisely is on the horizon. In my business I know what I'm doing next month and the month after. Beyond that, who knows?

In this challenging climate, change comes just like that. Technology has changed the way we all work, and we're facing competition not just from down the road, but from the other side of the planet. Projects and roles cross continents and industries and who knows what tomorrow will bring? An email in your in-box saying your role is being made redundant or an event that will present major opportunities for your role or business to excel – both are possibilities.

We live in tough times for doing business, for trading our craft, for earning a living. That backdrop gives us a challenge, but also an opportunity. Tough times call for survival tactics. For resilience, re-invention, flexibility and tenacity. As business models die and crumble, we need to innovate fresh ones. In an instant.

Survival is about being flexible and rapid but also embracing change, rather than seeing it as a threat.

A Juggler sees change as an opportunity not a crisis. Juggling is a valuable skill in an economic downturn because it's about:

! not putting all your eggs in one basket;

! being enterprising by having more than one skill set or trade;

! having the flexibility to integrate work and play.

Success might not rely on Survival Of The Fittest, but those who are most adept at juggling change.

Myth 2

'Success is about doing one thing'

'What do you want to be when you grow up?' goes the question.

From an early age we are encouraged to aspire to a single goal, growing up to do *one* job or have *one* trade. An electrician. A banker. A shopkeeper. Rarely a mix of disciplines. Society seems obsessed with the notion of doing one thing, of aspiring to do one job. I'd never thought it natural to do just one thing; it's so flawed.

That mindset starts at a young age when we are asked if we want to be a footballer, ballerina or paramedic when we grow up. Once you figure that one out, the education system opens your mind to the possibilities of new subjects and disciplines, before firmly shutting the door on them.

Like most of us in school, at 14 and 16 I made selections as to what subjects to study for the next two years. My heart chose Politics and Art (amongst others) but the system said I had to choose one or the other. I couldn't do both. A culture that doesn't reflect the broad personality or the rich texture of the individual seems flawed to me.

I was pleased to be liberated from the education system at 18 and took a class in photography and one in film studies, **at the same time** as working at a record shop **and** working in a radio station.

I enjoyed that year. 1986 was the year I learnt to juggle. Because life is not so black and white. Why is it one thing or the other? My peers either went out to work **or** went on to college; no-one mixed those up. What united it all for me? Stuff I was good at, and stuff I was passionate about. Going from college to the radio station one day; off at folk festivals selling records at the weekend.

Isn't this a more realistic model? Doesn't plurality more accurately reflect the fullness of who we are as human beings? Doesn't it better reflect the fragmented nature of 21st century society?

Workers have been forced to embrace that plurality as organisations and working dynamics change. Even in more traditional jobs, people are increasingly working on projects outside their core jobs. More than ever, it's about doing more than one thing.

The wine guru (amongst his other talents) Gary Vaynerchuk may have predicted he'd follow his father into running the family wine business, but he may not have anticipated he'd use that as a platform for having a daily online video show or that he'd have a reputation for a load of other stuff as well. What drives him is his passion for lots of interests from The Jets football team to social networking.

> *'We've become a society that feels that people need to be one-dimensional and one-trick ponies.'*

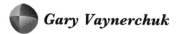 *Gary Vaynerchuk*

So whatever you do, don't be a one-trick pony – be multi-dimensional. And remember, doing more is not a headache; it's an opportunity.

Myth 3

'Specialism wins'

'Jack of All Trades, and Master of None' says the myth. Who says you can only be great at one thing and only be 'Jack' at others?

Sure, absolute total perfection takes a total 100% focus. I doubt Barack Obama or Tiger Woods would have succeeded if they were trying to achieve other big goals simultaneously. But in business and in life, sure you can be good – no, great – at loads of things.

It's all about Focus and Passion: if you apply those to everything you want to achieve, you don't need to limit yourself to one thing.

Let me remind you – here's how things used to be:

A writer was just a writer.
A designer was just a designer.

But now it's all mixed up. Because if you don't limit yourself, you can then realise your full potential.

A graphic designer I know is also a barman (he does both very well).
A photographer is also an arts festival organiser (ditto).

A writer is also a life coach.

A PR executive is also a psychology student.

So rethink Specialism. Who said Bob Dylan couldn't be a painter as well as a singer-songwriter? The talented musician Gilberto Gil is also a politician as Brazil's Minister of Culture. And Arnold Schwarzenegger has proved with his acting, bodybuilding and political talents that Renaissance Man is back. For Sean Coombs (aka P. Diddy) a career in the music industry wasn't enough so he added acting, TV and film production, restaurants and fashion to his portfolio. He is now a man of many hats – businessman, designer, producer, musician, actor, and philanthropist. You can't describe these guys with a one-word job title!

If you settle for narrow specialism, you'll close the door on a whole load of other opportunities both in terms of personal fulfillment and career potential. It's more important to approach life with some generic tools in your toolbox that you can apply to a variety of disciplines.

As CEO Worldwide of one of the largest creative organisations in the world, Kevin Roberts sees the value of people with that breadth.

'This whole notion of specialization vs. generalization I believe is a crock. It limits people. In my experience, people are much more capable than their specialty might suggest.

*Indeed to only focus on specialization leaves
a good deal of man's potential unrealized.*

*I like to hire great people with great atti-
tudes and we look for competitive, passionate, restless people focused on ideas who can
play on a team.*

It doesn't sound very specialized, does it?"

 Kevin

Myth 4

'Generalisation is bland'

Just because we know a lot of stuff doesn't mean we have
no substance. That breadth has value.

Generalists are often able to speak a universal language
translating the jargon of specialism. Think of them as
translators; people who can talk the right language to
clients, to the marketplace.

That aptitude for being a translator has commercial value.
As founder of her own new media business, Roxanne
Darling may be seen as an internet specialist but she likes
to focus her talents as someone who can bridge that gap

between specialism and the marketplace at large. Her business is about making the power of new media relevant to clients; she positions herself as a *'tour guide in the foreign country that is the Internet'*.

> *'I think being a translator of technology to business and vice versa is truly the strength of our company. Specialists are important but if you do not have generalists who can walk and talk back and forth between programming and marketing, or between builder and buyer, then too often there is confusion and conflict.'*

 *Roxanne Darling*

Generalists can also prove to be truly innovative because they have the vision to look across borders, to mix up completely disparate disciplines, breaking the rules in ways experts might not think of doing.

One example of a rule breaker who's 'looking across borders' is technology innovator David Prior of Prior Intelligence, who I recently met in London. Rather than just immerse himself in technical disciplines at the exclusion of other considerations, he sees himself as a generalist on the cusp of different areas of expertise. He's a 'Technology/Commercial Hybrid'. Whilst there are many technology specialists out there, there are not so many who mix their deep technological know-how with commercial strategy. His strength to the market is in occupying that middle ground, putting people together, connecting disparate disciplines, applying for example, biology to information exploitation.

'I tend to be driven purely by coffee and curiosity. To get to a point where you can understand lots of different things and you can apply them in lots of different ways … and where you're prepared to ignore the rules and to be passionate about it — is everything.'

David Prior

That desire for curiosity drives a business portfolio with no limits, where he mixes up whatever he fancies. Generalists are sometimes described as 'T-Shaped' people; they have a key skill set (that is the vertical leg of the T) but are accomplished at other stuff, they are flexible and knowledgeable in other disciplines. I take the 'T' in another direction as X-Shaped people who are talented at loads of stuff.

Mike Southon as entrepreneur, writer, motivational speaker, performer and mentor also has that breadth as a generalist. But he believes generalism can still be based on a single identity.

'Be very varied, but in one personality type. Within who you are you have incredible flexibility.'

 **Mike Southon**

So cross-pollinate and enrich yourself. Think like a poly-math and celebrate your breadth.

Myth 5

'If you want to be good in business, consult the rule book first'

One reason we can do so much more, juggle new stuff and launch new ventures in work and business is because so many barriers to entry have crumbled.

Want to set up a creative agency? All you need is a couple of freelancers, a website and a flipchart. Want to start video podcasting? Start now, this afternoon. Want to launch an internet business in your spare time? Everyone's doing it, and there's no rule book.

So many people have hobby businesses. I met a sales guy last year who has a website selling fridge magnets in his spare time; a couple I know are setting up a holiday let business. How many new mothers do you know who have part-time internet businesses selling baby clothes or jewellery? There are stacks of people planning their business on a napkin or the back of a beer mat, running businesses from their attics and spare rooms.

Because you **can** have a day job and a hobby business in your spare time. You just need passion, commitment and the ability to 'put in the hours'. You can take a small business into new markets. You can do the unthinkable. And this gives some great opportunities for juggling.

A guy I know has a day job, but also does freelance design jobs, runs an eBay business with his wife and manages a holiday let by the coast. Because he can. Because he's enterprising and because there are no rules.

He's not really doing it for the money. He's doing it because he loves it like that. And because setting up a new business in 2009 doesn't necessarily need bricks and mortar offices or investor funding. Instead you need tenacity, passion and the balls to go for it.

Myth 6

'Work is done in an office'

'The traditional distinction between leisure and work is becoming increasingly blurred. People do not stop thinking just because they leave the office. Ideas are processed in our dreams. The development also makes the classical distinction between home and office less relevant. In the blurred society, work is no longer a place – it is an activity.'

Kjell Nordstrom and Jonas Ridderstrale, Funky Business*

People work in ever-changing ways. Businesses are run from coffee shops, projects are outsourced to the developing world, and virtual working by virtual teams is increasingly commonplace. I just had conversations on the phone with two clients. One was in his car in Abu Dhabi; the other walking his dogs along the beach in the UK. And that's how we do business. Work is not a place you go, it's what you do, it's part of your DNA.

So don't measure productivity by how long you're at your desk; you can do it anywhere. Flexible working or working

---

* *Funky Business* by Kjell Nordstrom and Jonas Ridderstrale (*Financial Times*/Prentice Hall 2001).

from home is not a doss. It's being smart enough to know how and where you work best. Of where you get results. Of where you really rock 'n' roll with ideas and achievement. Employers need to trust that results will be delivered. Because if you think that working from home is about sitting with your feet up and watching Jerry Springer then – unless it is a particularly inspiring episode – that won't get results.

I was out for a day of meetings and put an auto responder on my email saying 'I am out of the office'. *'What do you mean, you are out of the office?'* shouted back a reply from my friend David, *'YOU ARE YOUR OFFICE.'*

And he's right; work is no longer somewhere we clock in and out of; it's a mindset that we dip in and out of.

That redefining of work is going to take a lot of getting used to for some people. When I went to get my hair cut last Monday, the new hairdresser asked, *'Not working today?'* Then I was on my way to meet with a designer, wearing shorts and a t-shirt. A friend saw me walking to the train. *'Day off today?'* she asked.

And it's only a little something, but it's a commentary on how some people still perceive work. To them, 'work' = you wear a suit, you are chained to a desk all day (and you would only get your hair cut on a day off). Some of us have freedom to choose. When we work. Where we work. How we work, what we wear and yes, even when we get our hair cut.

Just because this is how our parents' generation did things does not mean we have to do the same.

> **'Do not get trapped into the business of doing business, the bureaucracy, or the way things were done before.**
>
> **This is a new century, a new world.'**

 Kevin

André Balazs is a Manhattan-based hotelier responsible for some of the most celebrated hotels in the US, including Hollywood's Chateau Marmont and New York's Mercer.

> *'My perfect weekend is … just like the rest of my week,* ***a healthy dose of work and play.*** *I no longer separate the week from the weekend;* ***I now … just consider my briefcase to be the office.'***

André Balazs*

---

*   'My Perfect Weekend', *Financial Times*, 1 September 2007.

Myth 7

'Productivity = hours worked'

The traditional indicator for productivity is the number of hours an executive works. Like the factory clocking-in/clocking-out model, of course it is hopelessly flawed.

It's just – did you finish the task, did you deliver that project, make that sale, exceed expectations? It's not *where* you did it, or *what hours* you worked. It's just about results. Every time.

So the bottom line is your contribution. That's what the organisation wants and that's what you should be measured by.

The more talented you are the more choices you should be able to make, the more control you have. Remember that an employer would usually always rather retain talent than lose it. So if you want to take a sabbatical, if you want to work Wednesdays at home, if you need to leave the office at 17:30 to get home to see your kids, if you're good – or more likely if you're bloody good – sure, why not? You are paid for your ideas, performance and achievements not the hours you sit at your desk.

Times are changing and successful corporations are creating working environments where executives are not only encouraged to juggle but are also offered flexibility in working practices to do their own thing, to work from home, to take two Fridays off a month, whatever. Some companies are introducing *ROWE*, a results-only-work-environment where you won't be judged by the hours spent at your desk or cubicle. You *can* take that time out for your kid's concert; you *can* get your hair done on a Monday morning. So if you've done your work, quit the office!

A results-only system can revolutionise organisations as they are opened up to more honesty. No-one is hiding behind their partition pretending to be at work, or struggling to be at their desk at 08:30 just for the sake of it. Companies who have implemented it find that the lack of clock-watching and the trust instilled with their workforce means not only productivity rises but so does morale. It's win–win.

This is at odds with how things used to be. Ten years ago I had a job offer from a big corporation who said working at home was not part of the culture. The HR Manager explained the culture was you *will* be in the office at 08:00 and you *will* stay until 18:30. I'm not shy of working hard and producing great results but not with such rigid rules. I turned them down. More recently, another company I worked with seemed obsessed by measuring performance through similar indicators. An executive who was at her desk at 08:30 and left at 18:30 without leaving her post was viewed as a loyal and productive staff member regardless of what she actually did all day.

But it's actually what you did today, what difference you made. That's where the value is. How good an ambassador were you for the company, how did that meeting go, what was that margin on the sale you made, how is morale in the team you lead, how many make-a-difference ideas did you come up with today?

Those answers are the only ones that count.

It's a bit like how I work as a consultant, running my own business. Whilst I still work with clients on an 'on the clock' timesheet basis, I prefer to value my worth on how effective my ideas and services are. Staff productivity should be measured as though they are independent contractors or suppliers – on results and performance.

That's how the real market works.

Myth 8

'It's all about the money'

Our society places so much emphasis on material status and wealth. But is success really just about the money? Don't people strive to do what they love, rather than to earn loads of money?

Many people I know who earn loads of money seem to hanker for a dream job to escape their corporate mediocrity. They're seeking an exit. People want meaning in their life, they want fulfilment.

A model that only places value on a salary package is flawed because what's the point of being an unhappy rich executive? Wouldn't you rather be rich in other ways: quality of life, variety and stimulation?

With demanding jobs, growing mortgages and young kids, many of us feel stressed. But there is a choice. If you work 14-hour days and are unhappy, do something different. TAKE CONTROL! Downsize, and benefit from a job that you enjoy more.

Sure, we all need enough money to pay the bills. But try removing making money as your primary motivator. The more passionate you are the more successful you'll be.

Because if you love what you do, you'll work harder, be more productive and can enjoy more success.

It's having the guts to quantify your job by more important criteria than money alone.

Myth 9

'A job is for life'

Work patterns and organisations are changing radically. The idea that workers have one fixed job is becoming an old-fashioned notion as people have embraced new disciplines and responsibilities.

In our parents' generation, people strived for a job for life, a single specialism working for one employer: that was the goal! Now the goal is to be more promiscuous, sacrificing that job security in exchange for values like autonomy and flexibility. I can't imagine a Job For Life, because it sounds like a life sentence. Unless I had the freedom to constantly change and re-invent, I would hate things standing still. I could not survive a culture of such little change.

Things are different now. The power is vested in the individual as she chooses what she wants to do, how she wants to do it, and if the organisation can't give her that, then she moves on.

The bottom line is that you can call the shots if you are good at what you do. In a crowded and competitive job market, there is power in the Juggler.

Career development is not just filling a role; it's growing and developing a role. Even when I was in a proper job, I had many simultaneous hats, some of which I had chosen for myself. That may be tough to pull off when you start out in the job market, but the more you achieve, the more control you have. You can seek to carve out your own role, a mix of what you want and working practices to suit. That's what gives you value.

You don't need to stay within the confines of a job title; if you have a contribution to bring to other parts of the business or organisation, start extending your talents. Start with a job spec and review and transform it. Grasp the opportunity and take a role in your required direction, ticking off your personal goals on the journey. And there's nothing wrong with being promiscuous in your personal development: finding new organisations, products, brands and teams to belong to, projects to run and products to get passionate about before you move on to the next thing.

The emphasis is on keeping yourself stimulated, motivated and happy – not earning your gold watch for 30 years' long service. With 'job security' a distant and outdated notion, there won't be many 'jobs for life' around anyway.

Myth 10

'Your job title counts'

Why does everyone want to know what it says on your business card? Why do people want to put their job titles on their email footers? People get obsessed by titles. Some guys who used to work for me would rather have 'Manager' or 'Head Of' in their job title than a pay rise. But pigeon-holing can be misleading. A woman who works in Operations but is also adept at sales and marketing is labelled 'The Operations Woman'.

The reality of career development is that it tends to be more organic than strategic. We fall into roles because opportunities arise. The danger is that those fallen-into roles start to define us, and become labels for how outsiders perceive us. And you need to break out of those labels.

At the start of my television career there was an opening in post-production, the editing side of TV. Editing wasn't my love or passion but I saw an opportunity to leave my apprenticeship as 'a runner', so I took it. The danger

was that people who didn't know my breadth and skill
sets saw me as *just* the Post-Production Guy. Fortunately,
one of my mentors had the wisdom to see me as a
Safe Pair Of Hands* who could do lots of stuff and he
whisked me off to a new venture he was launching.
Next I was Event Co-ordinator who also headed up
marketing, helping out on site and mastering the lami-
nating machine, together with hands-on production,
budgeting, bits of everything. And that whetted my
appetite to be a Juggler.

A similar kind of pigeon-holing reappeared at my next
job when I entered the company as a co-ordinator running
a radio studio, rising to be its Managing Director. So now
Ian was seen as *just* The Studio Guy. I had to embark on
a personal PR crusade to show that I could be thrown
just about anything and soon I was given other non-studio
projects to run – but I had to fight those misperceptions
along the way. I asked to get involved in other projects
and areas that interested me. I dreamt up job titles: '*Special
Projects Manager*' became a euphemism for sweeping up
loads of bits and pieces in a single portfolio. I relished
that diverse mix. All my colleagues had straight, fixed
jobs (apart from the CEO, of course). But I'd carved out
an idiosyncratic role; one that would have people scratch-
ing their heads asking '*what does Ian Sanders actually do?*'

---

* *I was considered to be a Safe Pair Of Hands as I was good at photocopying and
going to Oddbins on a Friday night to pick up some bottles of Australian sparkling wine
(essential skills in TV in 1990).*

This breadth was a perfect learning experience for my next role of taking the leap to start my own business.

During my time with that company, they introduced a no-job-titles rule for business cards. It was actually more about egalitarianism than a move away from being defined by a title; but either way, our personal brands became more important.

I had such a mixed self-invented portfolio, the company struggled to replace me when I quit, as no-one could quite replicate all the stuff I did. Which is a great goal to have.

Seek to carve out a very You portfolio or role, not based on a job title, but based on your abilities, passions, what you're good at.

Myth 11

'Keep family out of it!'

Let's face it, whatever the assurances of recruitment ads where employers might promise 'to put families first', when push comes to shove they won't put your family ahead of the organisation. So you need to make sure you do, and factor it in to your juggling.

Some of us juggle because we need to mix up work with family responsibilities. We have babies, kids or grandkids who we need to integrate into our lives, we want to become super-adept at gear-shifting, juggling some very different sorts and shapes of balls.

Lots of us have become skilled at segueing seamlessly from nappy changing to budget changing, from conference call to bedtime story. We juggle projects, roles and business with bringing up a family. And it can be tough.

But it's all a matter of planning. Whether you are a return-to-work Mum, working part-time, or a Dad who's decided to share childcare with his partner, it can be challenging, so you might need to get some principles in place. When I work at home I get to see my young children. But you need to have rules. When Daddy is in the office and the door is shut, it means 'do not disturb'. Mostly, it works.

But what about the upsides. Daddy can have lunch with the children. When I was working at home last week I cycled into town, bought some fresh fish, came back and cooked it for us for lunch. That felt great. You can even create little windows of play throughout the day; taking a 10-minute 'timeout' to play football with my two-year-old is priceless. Sure, it can get confusing. 20 seconds from client call to kick-around and back again. But if you get organised, it's all very do-able.

Integrating family might be one of your more challenging juggles, but it's probably one of the most rewarding.

Entrepreneur and *Financial Times* Columnist Luke Johnson observed that 21st-century entrepreneurs are the first generation of male executives whose hobbies are families, not drinking.

> '(They) can not only close a sale or raise venture capital but they can also change a nappy, baby-sit and talk knowledgably about schools and exams. I'm not alone in regularly slipping out of the office early to be home in time for the children's bath and a bedtime story.'

*Luke Johnson**

Becoming a parent also has a healthy, life-orienting impact, putting all your 'work worries' into perspective. It reminds us what's *really* important.

If you can succeed in integrating work and family effectively – in contrast to our parents' generation where such things were at arms-length – then you'll get some real benefits from juggling.

---

* *Financial Times*, 24 June 2008.

Myth 12

'In search of the eternal work/life balance'

The problem with the term 'Work/Life Balance' is that it implies a calm equilibrium between your personal life and your work life; but of course, it's anything but. It's more likely to be all over the bloody place!

There's no neat divide between home and work. When you're working, you still think of personal stuff, and when you're not at work – in the shower, in the car, doing the shopping – that's when you'll have clarity for problem solving or thoughts for topping up your to-do list. As technology and flexibility enable '*Martini*' working ('Anytime, Anyplace, Anywhere'), then it's more blurred than ever as we work from home, from our beds, cafés, holidays and all those traditional non-work spaces.

People entering the job market now – what has been billed 'Generation Y' – have different priorities; they are striving for flexible working and that quality of life rather than salary or status. This generation is more promiscuous in the job market than its predecessors. These people are not in search of a job for life. They know what they want and how they want it; they are challenging common perceptions on work. They are creating a new work ethic.

Some think that our obsession with work/life is a fad, but it's misunderstood. Work/life balance is a red herring; it's actually about integration. Of loving what you do, which means you'll be more passionate, work harder and have more fun.

Some employers approach these themes with good intentions but work/life balance is such a hot topic, there's a danger that organisations are banding around these buzzwords, making hollow proclamations. I browsed the job ads in a Sunday paper. One employer stood out in its recruitment ad: 'work/life balance is important and families come first'. Another promised, 'we follow flexible working practices, which enables employees to have two Fridays off per month'.

But having two Fridays off is not really the point. It needs to be part of a bigger picture, of a whole new mindset of work, of contributions to organisations. This is not about wearing jeans to the office on a Friday or having more holidays.

Work/Play *integration* is the future. Combining your passions and talents in one package.

Myth 13

'You have to stick with the status quo'

I'm fed up hearing people say they're unhappy in their job when I know they can do something about it. If you are talented then have the balls and courage to re-style your life and become a Juggler. Don't prostitute yourself to the organisation and turn tricks in return for a payslip.

Remember, it doesn't have to be all or nothing. You don't have to quit your day job in insurance for a life on the farm. Instead, focus on re-framing your job and re-aligning your priorities and desires.

Try changing your organisational portfolio, or maybe spending less time at your desk. From job-shares to flexible working, there are options to consider for different working practices.

If you're self employed your working life may better lend itself to juggling. Because then there really are no rules. Nick is an IT Systems advisor, a consultant to big corporations. But he also manages rock bands and writes music (mostly for love, not money). James is a designer but also co-manages a bar. He also has the flexibility to hang out with his kids and tend an allotment when he's not at his Mac or behind a bar.

But whether you work for someone else or if you're your own boss, don't settle for a work life that's mediocre. And don't settle for a work life where you become addicted to work.

Juggling can be the route out of being a workaholic; getting a better mix of work and play. We've all done it. Got sucked into our jobs so we become a one-trick pony, narrow in our focus. Work. Work. Work. That'll make you stressed and unhappy (and not forgetting dull). And you can risk burn out.

Eight years ago I did exactly that and became depressed. I was thinking of quitting. My boss said take three weeks off and sit on a beach in Thailand. It was a nice gesture but it was too late. The damage was done. I needed the beach six weeks earlier, but I was too busy with my head down to notice. I needed to mix things up a bit, do more of what I enjoyed, and hire a deputy or two. Instead I quit. With retrospect other options were available.

It's a similar story for a friend of mine. He was also stressed and unhappy so decided to leap from his corporate job to a new venture. One day in a team, in an infrastructure, with a corporate mission. The next, just him and his laptop at home. Pretty extreme. He'd spent his career in big corporations; he'd never worked for himself. A radical move (and nothing wrong with radical moves). But how about he'd mixed it up? Two days a week working for his old company; three days per week doing his own thing? Why does it always have to be so black and white? You can have a powerful job and enjoy loads of success OR you retire early to live in France and spend your life playing tennis. But it's not always a question of one thing or the other.

People get stressed and pressured into making those big black and white decisions – when they should pause and consider The Third Option.

That third option is **Living The Juggle Life**. ...

Part Two

REDESIGN YOUR LIFE: THINK 'JUGGLE'!

In 1994, the management guru Tom Peters wrote *Crazy Times Call For Crazy Organisations*.* He was right. Now we live in even crazier times. And these times call for Jugglers.

If you challenge those old assumptions of work, this is a world where you can be defined by who you really are rather than by a single job title. There are no rules to career development – you can carve out a unique role wrapping up your passions and interests.

You can factor in to your Juggle life everything that drives, inspires and stimulates you. Whether that be people, places, goals, mindsets or whatever.

When you do that *and* get paid for it, life feels good. A life where you segue from play to work and back again. Work is not drudgery, work becomes you.

---

* *The Tom Peters Seminar: Crazy Times Call for Crazy Organizations* by Tom Peters (Vintage Books, May 1994).

Forget labels and corporate status; success is now down to the right attitude and those all important juggling skills. You only live once. If you hate your job, change your relationship with work; it doesn't have to be a case of all or nothing. View a multi-dimensional work life as a positive force, as laying some great foundation stones for a new life that can give you variety, stimulation, flexibility and success. Just think: what an amazing opportunity …

Juggling is being your own business strategist whilst choosing to stay in control of your own destiny. You can embrace a new mindset to change your life. Rather than working harder, it's about working *smarter*, doing what you love and what you are good at. It's not a question of reclaiming time; but more a case of reclaiming your life.

> '*It all starts with my long held belief that work/life balance is an outdated concept. Oprah Winfrey has the right approach, "Live your best life every day". So when asked, as I was recently by Fortune about work/life balance, it's simply the wrong question. The right question is work/life integration. How do you integrate work, family, fun, community, and social commitment into one passionate day, week, month, year, life?*'

 Kevin

1

Set your personal Sat Nav

As I sat having my morning espresso today, a flyer in my local coffee shop caught my eye. It was advertising a Life Coach and proclaimed '*Create the life you've always wanted*' and '*Start living your dreams*'. We are bombarded by messages that encourage us to get empowered and fulfilled but too often we think we're too damn busy to take action. So make sure you do something.

Firstly, you need to work out where you are now and where you are seeking to go. Do you yearn for a bigger playing field? Are you locked into a single-discipline organisational culture or mentality where if you seek to go off into another area you're accused of straying off the ball? Then it is time to make a change.

Becoming a Juggler is about re-aligning your work life to tick your personal boxes. It could be a radical change; or it could be small changes. I heard of an executive who decided to quit his job to start anew. He felt he needed to '*hit control-alt-delete*' and start all over again. But you don't always need a total re-boot to shake things up.

If you're not happy, reset your Sat Nav. Ask yourself how you want your work life to change. You don't have to be freaked out by envisaging that change in one huge leap; instead think small 'salami' steps. What are salami steps? Think of achieving change slice by slice; it can be easier that way.

Becoming a Juggler is about being brave and avoiding getting stuck in a rut. You might have material success but do you have stuff that counts, like quality of life and health?

You need self-confidence and stacks of self-belief to bespoke the life you want and empower yourself that it's all possible. Because without that, you won't get anywhere.

So you have to:

! know what you want;

! AND believe you can get there.

Then it's just a matter of going for it.

Having a destination in mind is really valuable. Five years ago on holiday in Turkey I articulated such a goal. I was working for myself but was unhappy. I wasn't stimulated enough, I felt isolated and I wasn't earning enough money. I knew what I wanted, but didn't know how I'd get there. In an old notepad I found the other day, I'd written back then as a goal, '*Design a portfolio lifestyle*'.

And I have achieved it. It took a while to reach that goal. Sometimes by design, mostly by default. But I arrived at my destination. And it feels good.

If you're sitting there thinking your life is not what you want and you can't see how you can change it, think of those small steps to re-engineer your work life.

And start now:

- **!** Take on a new project as stage one on your journey to become multi-dimensional.

- **!** Change your working hours.

- **!** Look for a new job with an employer whose culture reflects your own personality.

- **!** Learn a foreign language in your lunch break.

Do something – anything – to break up the tedium of your job so it's more about you. Start slicing.

2

Become your very own architect

Once you've chosen to live a Juggle Life you are the architect of your own destiny. You decide what the foundation stones are of your juggle life. You choose what's in and what's out. Whether you are going to re-shape your job or carve out a brand new role and identity, the power is in your ability to choose what you want to do. Keep your options open as you make choices and decisions as to how you can carve up your life. Don't be restricted by thinking you can only have a single professional offering.

> *'It's the only way I ever saw it – my DNA makes me a Juggler, and I embrace my DNA. I think there are way too many Jugglers out there trying to be dentists and vice versa. I think we all have a little juggle in us and I hope that everybody embraces it.'*

 Gary

If you are open-minded to take on more stuff, you'll be rewarded with variety.

Variety has multiple benefits:

! It will enrich you.

! It makes you enterprising.

! It's in your DNA to be multi-dimensional; you can get involved in lots of different stuff.

! You don't want to restrict yourself; you can be more than a one-trick pony.

! It's recession-proof. One hat or business model fails, you have others to fall back on.

! It will inevitably be boredom-busting.

But there's something more critical here. By being your own architect, you have the potential for greater success because you can be true to yourself, do what you want. No rules. And that is very liberating.

Rejoice in being your very own architect, creating a unique lifestyle. What an opportunity. You look around and genuinely feel the world is your oyster. And that is a fantastically empowering feeling.

3

Enjoy living a blur

Now you're a Juggler, Work = Life, they're all mixed up.

For me, it's what comes naturally, it's what I am. Sitting in a quiet moment on holiday and not thinking about my next book or a great business idea is anathema. It was such a moment on a holiday that I had the idea for my first book, *Leap!*

There are challenges in blurring these boundaries between work and play. In the Old Days, 'Home' was about family and 'Work' was a building you walked into Monday to Friday. In between was a drive or a train ride. You read the paper on the train in; you fell asleep on the way back. These were the punctuation marks for your working day, all neatly segmented. That's where you placed work.

Well the Old Days are over.

Chances are you work at home sometimes. Chances are you at least think of work (if not 'do' work) at evenings and weekends.

If you're on *Facebook*, you're used to merging work and play. Your network of contacts embraces friends, family, co-workers and clients. Your identity is all mixed up. The same with *Twitter* as you tweet on everything from your latest meeting to that gig you went to last night. Not only do *Twitter* and *Facebook* cross the divide between home and work, so do activities like blogging when you write a narrative of your thoughts and what you are up to. Where do you categorise that? Is it work or play? Answer – It's just me.

For some, the screen you work at is also the screen you play at; we use a personal computer for work and play. That can get confusing. As I type away, am I at work or at play? Reading emails from friends, uploading photos to share, watching TV shows on the iPlayer, online banking, listening to iTunes. That convergence of work and play through one device with no separation is a metaphor for our juggle-shaped lives.

When you work from home it can get even more confusing as there are no buffers, none of those punctuation marks in the day. One Friday I finished a meeting at 4pm and then met my wife and son for a coffee before walking home. Once home I checked my emails and sent off a proposal to a client. I then played with my son before making a phone call and dealing with a query on a project. Then I gave my son a bath, put him to bed, checked my emails whilst I poured a glass of wine and guests arrived for dinner. The end of the day was totally seamless, there was no punctuation between 'work' and 'play'. And that afternoon I have described is far from unique; it's what hundreds of thousands of us do all over the world every day of their lives.

It can be difficult with those blurs but, if you love what you do, 'working' in playtime is not so much of a chore.

4

Corporate juggling

Employers are starting to change their organisations to embrace the Juggle spirit. Companies like Google and 3 m encourage 'what if?' thinking by giving workers one day a week – so called 'slack time' – to develop projects of their own, whilst employers like Innocent Drinks encourage an idiosyncratic culture where the personality of the individual is preserved and personal development is encouraged. St Luke's, the progressive UK advertising agency founded by Andy Law, was one of the pioneers in putting personal development first, with its staff active stakeholders in the firm. Here workers eschewed traditional work environments to hot-desk and have meetings in corridors, coffee shops, wherever. St Luke's offered staff a 'Make Yourself More Interesting Fund', a budget to fund extra-curricular stuff its staff wanted to do. The company did everything but play by the rules.

'Work like this is scary as hell. But you are twenty first century pioneers, interconnected and learning all the time. You are also individuals whose work life has the capacity to be as surprising as you fancy.'

Andy Law, Founder of St Luke's*

As companies strive to win accolades as the nation's best place to work, more and more organisations are offering Jugglers perfect environments to incubate their talents; where they can carve out juggle-shaped lives with flexible working, autonomy, empowerment and even sabbaticals along the way.

'We try to provide four things to all our people at Saatchi & Saatchi: Responsibility, Learning, Recognition and Joy. I look for the same four things in everything I do. It's not about command and control; it's about unleash and inspire.'

 Kevin

Many big corporations provide paid sabbaticals to long-standing employees; rewarding them with 10 weeks off after 10 years' service. Whilst that is out of the reach of most small businesses, more organisations are looking at offering career breaks whether to reward loyal staff or

---

*   *Experiment at Work: Explosions and Experiences at the Most Frightening Company on Earth* by Andy Law (Profile Books, 2003).

benefit from reinvigorated personal contributions. Kevin Roberts thinks everyone should have 40-day sabbaticals written into their contracts *'to improve and liberate themselves'*. He funds two teachers a year at his old school, Lancaster Royal Grammar School, to do just that, *'because I believe they come back as better people'*.

The future is about workers thinking and acting like entrepreneurs, whatever their organisational culture.

5

Celebrate your multi-dimensional talents

Many executives have managed to create their own portfolios by mixing skills, roles or even jobs. Others have hobby interests or business interests on the side.

I know Jugglers who mix stuff up. A business consultant who chose to work three days a week when she returned to work after having kids. A woman who works two shifts a week producing radio shows; the rest of the time she produces her kids' lives. An HR Manager three days a week who makes jewellery and organises arts events when she is not sorting out employment contracts. A headhunter who has a side-job playing in a band that he hires out to his day-job clients. Mixing up his passions. By day the *BlackBerry*, by night a very different kind of keyboard.

The reality is that most of us have a plurality of talents to match our plurality of tastes. Look at anyone's iPod track listing – we do listen to hip hop *and* classical music; we do watch 'The Simpsons' *and* period dramas; we like 'Atonement' *and* the 'Sex and the City' movie. It's a not a case of either/or. We are multi-faceted. That is part of our personality and our richness informs our professional tastes, portfolios and abilities.*

In a post on his website Gary Vaynerchuk observed how he was getting lots of comments from people surprised that he was knowledgeable about technology as well as wine.

> *'... And I gave that a lot of thought. How people are branded and pigeon holed into being able to do one thing. I don't think people realise – we are multi-dimensional people. I know about the Jets, I know about wine, I know about cheese and tea and other things. And yes I know about business and philosophy. Yes I have built a lot of businesses.'*

 Gary

---

* *so don't even think about categorising me ...*

That plurality is not just driven by our tastes and passions. There are also good economic reasons to have broad talents. A business with multiple products generating multiple revenue streams or an executive with strengths in more than one area have the potential to be more recession proof.

If tough market conditions threaten the viability of one activity or skill, you can migrate to another. Because if they are getting rid of Operations people but you also 'do' R&D, then that can help you survive. You are less disposable. A friend of mine qualified as an accountant but, rather than just stay in finance, he migrated to become a general manager, commercial director, and then a CEO. His financial skills are very much part of his DNA but he's a broader animal. And compare that with his peers from accounting class who have stuck to finance.

It's like when I was MD of a division of a group. I ran other (unrelated) projects for the group at the same time because I could — and more importantly — because I wanted to. My predecessor just filled the MD post and stopped at that. But why stop there when you have no boundaries? Consider how much more value this offers the employer, they get two jobs done for the price of one.

So it's a matter of Narrow Focus Vs Breadth.

I know who I'd rather have in my team.

6

Be the real you

I confess: I'm really mixed-up.

In a working day, my projects can range from an assignment for a Fortune 500 company to working for a one-person start-up. Business advice, marketing services, project management. Yes, it's eclectic.

A client asked me about my competitors. I don't have easily-comparable competitors because no-one quite has the mix I do. That's what makes me unique. A marketing advisor, project manager, strategist, micro-entrepreneur who can also write copy, write books and advise on a whole load of other things beside.

My portfolio of business services is not informed by conventional definition or market positioning. It's simpler than that. My services and the eclectic mix of what I do is driven by me. It's a reflection of who I am.

The 'old me' was sometimes shy of communicating that breadth to clients because they might have seen that as a weakness. Now I am prouder of who I am, clients know that they get value from that breadth and experience. It's what defines me. My business self is my personality. A client asked if I could copywrite some marketing materials. That wasn't my core discipline, but sure. It was an interesting client and I was stimulated by the challenge. The client got a whole load of extra value because I have those other strings to my bow. Ideas, input and contacts I can bring to his project = added value for him. Proof that breadth has tangible commercial value in the market.

Decide what you'd like in your portfolio and try to create it. I wanted to get involved in the local arts and creative community plus I wanted to 'give something back' so I worked *pro bono* for a local art event. It brought me stimulation and a good bunch of people to be involved with. So whether your passion is art or football, creative writing or helping disadvantaged kids, build it in to your life.

Let your personality shape your business offering; to everyone you interact with across work, play, clients, boss, teams and family, 24/7 – you can be THE REAL YOU.

What a relief … !

7

Playing it your way

When you're living the Juggle life, you can take control of what you do. You can make choices of what you do and how you do it.

There is so much emphasis on having power in a job. Swap power for choice and you'll have greater job satisfaction. Forget climbing the career ladder and traditional status. Work out what really matters. Think of the benefits of career breaks, changes in direction and doing it your way. And if you work for the right kind of employer, they'll be keen to offer you such autonomy because they know the value of a happy executive versus an unhappy one.

A friend works for a big corporation. After 10 years climbing the ladder he now heads a division. He's built himself a corporate ecosystem – not unlike a small business of his own – that gives him what he wants and what he needs. Sure, he has big responsibility and pressures, but also the support infrastructure to delegate to and help out. He travels a lot, but ensures his family doesn't suffer from a busy schedule. Wherever possible he flies out on a Monday evening and returns overnight on a Thursday so he can work at home Monday and Friday and see his kids. Where appropriate, he might take his family with him on some trips. He runs a successful business unit but juggles it well with personal priorities. In the business he keeps an overview, dipping in to what he wants (and what he needs to), leaving some stuff to people who'll do it better.

He juggles staff, clients, agendas, family, time zones and schedules. But he's in control, making choices about what to do. And in doing so, he's doing it His Way. He can afford to do that – and is permitted to – because he's good at what he does and he gets the right results (that simple).

How do you get in a position to do it your way?

! Get a reputation for being good.

! As you grow and take on more responsibilities, recruit support staff who you can delegate to.

! Work hard but be bold and confident enough to say you'll only do it your way.

In return for your commitment and loyalty, you are rewarded with quality of life and autonomy.

Sounds like a fair deal to me!

Sure, be part of an organisation, be a team player, but redesign your working life to have it your way.

If you pull it off, you'll enjoy success, flexibility and autonomy.

8

Think constant re-invention

If you're striving for continued and improved success, there is one fact of life:

You can't stand still. You can't stop. You have to keep on moving.

Change comes from nowhere. Often we're forced to embrace changing business models, new market conditions, new products, threats from a competitor, whatever. So you have to change what you do or how you do it. Change a product or pricing strategy.

Our Juggler Mike Southon has a more proactive approach to change: he tries to pre-empt it, in a seven-year cycle, rather than just react to it.

Mike's had a varied career. After starting as a chemical engineer and a salesman selling scaffolding, then he founded several companies, became a successful entrepreneur, co-wrote some business books, started motivational speaking, wrote a column about it, podcast about it. That diversity has always driven Mike. But whatever he did, sometimes consciously, sometimes unconsciously, he developed a philosophy that whatever it is you do, you should think of changing it every seven years:

'You've got the seven year itch, it seems like the magic number; even if you have achieved success you may be essentially bored by what you are doing and people get trapped in that. So I try a mental exercise, at about seven years I just think, let's try something else. Certainly in seven years' time I know I'll be doing something different to what I'm doing now.'

 Mike

So embrace change and be prepared to re-invent what you do. Even if you stay working in the same corporate environment, try re-inventing yourself doing a number of jobs. In my seven years* in my last 'proper' job, I literally had 10 different jobs – learning, growing and carving out a unique role.

Re-invention is not a sign of being fickle; it's an essential part of personal and corporate development. But more importantly, it's actually about survival.

---

*   There we are, I – subconsciously – did the Seven Year Thing.

9

Being adept at gear shifting

Even ex-Prime Ministers are becoming Jugglers. By doing that, they realise their new life can give them all they want.

Tony Blair may have had a lot on his plate when he was Prime Minister, but he still had one job title on the door. Now he's left office he juggles a broad portfolio from Middle East peace envoy to consultant at JP Morgan. He also runs a development project for Africa, consults, speaks and runs two foundations in the UK, one focused on sport, the other on faith. He's become a portfolio worker. With his staff of 30, Blair equates his new multi-dimensional role to running a small business, constantly juggling, shifting gears from a phone call to the Middle East with a trip to a UK sports centre via breakfast with George W Bush.

Blair's agendas are big. And it doesn't get much bigger than peace in the Middle East, effortlessly segueing to the more trivial, whether to do that speaking engagement or not.

That constant gear shifting is what juggling is all about: reviewing, changing priorities, switching thoughts, agendas and tasks. One minute: huge stuff. The next minute: tiny stuff. In isolation, they make no sense. But the sum of the parts is one beautifully intricate jigsaw.

If you get stale working on one project or one assignment, the joy of doing other stuff simultaneously is that you can shift gears to something else, switching back later. This is a great way to manage projects because short bursts of energy and creative thought can be highly productive. Gear shifting creates fresh thought and even those eureka moments when you return to projects, or you might find you have snatches of genius in between stuff.

I was working on a big project one afternoon. In between meetings, I was reviewing some copy for a client brochure, up against a deadline. And my wife telephoned me. She was out shopping and said *'I know you're very busy but I've got an important question.'* Sure, I replied.

'Do I get Barney the Bob The Builder pants or the Roary The Racing Car ones?' she asked. Without missing a beat I responded, *'Get a pack of each.'*

And that decision may not have been peace in the Middle East but being part of the decision to choose our potty-training toddler's first pair of underpants was a seminal moment.

You'll get used to that juggling, hour by hour dealing with big stuff and little stuff. And often you'll have to go from low to high gears in a beat.

10

The importance of playtime

Some may think that an executive who has decided to leave the office early for the weekend, or go to the gym or golf course in the morning is 'taking it easy'.

But as the borders between work and play get blurred, those kind of distinctions aren't so simple any more. After all, 'play time' is a worker's best tool for drive and stimulation.*

Whether it's the shower, the run or having a coffee – that's when we have ideas, sparks of inspiration, consistently and effectively. And that's how – for me – work and play are interlinked, **not** neatly separated. I met a woman who is a regional manager in corporate banking, looking after relationships with small and medium-size businesses. Each morning you'll find her swimming at her health club. She works out of home and client offices most of the time, so takes advantage of flexibility where she can, disappearing to swim late morning whilst working at a spreadsheet at home in the evening. She feels she's mixing

---

* I have just been for a run along the seafront. More powerful than a double espresso for motivation.

up the benefits of her role with the flexibility of how she does it.

Mike Southon uses his regular Saturday run around Hampstead Heath to write his column. While he's getting the benefit of exercise, he's ticking off something from his to-do list at the same time.

So don't dismiss 'play time' as taking time off, or taking it easy. The effective juggling of integrating work and play time is fundamental to success and, just as we have re-thought 'Work', we also need to rethink 'Play'.

I was early for a meeting in Central London and had 20 minutes to spare. Rather than walk in to Prêt A Manger and boot up my laptop I looked across the street and went in to The National Portrait Gallery, where I browsed a photography exhibition. It was an inspiring and pleasant punctuation mark to the day; it took me 10 minutes.

At the end of the day living the Juggle life enables you to make choices as to what are the important things in life, so try and punctuate your day with some play.

11

Being authentic

Most of us have at one time sat in meetings, boardrooms, or job interviews and thought 'we don't fit in here', but inevitably put on a mask or put in a performance and just got on with the job in hand. There was this bloke who worked for me. He was good, hardworking and reliable but I rarely saw any passion on a day-to-day basis. But when he was talking about snowboarding or DJ-ing, then his passion really shone through. He loved it. Ironically, he was one step ahead of me. He set up a hobby business running snowboarding holidays and club nights. That was where his heart was, that was where the Real Him lay. Perhaps he should have migrated from his day job to that passion, who knows what he could have done with that business in taking it beyond a hobby?*

Juggling is having the confidence to carve out your own areas and proclaim 'this is who I am' regardless of perception and conforming to convention.

Mike Southon might look like different people to different clients. Newspaper Columnist, Writer, Entrepreneur, Performer. But behind it all he is the same person. He

---

* He's now taken that brand and set up his own business.

might turn his on-stage persona on and off but he never dilutes or compromises his personality. It's all the same Mike.

Mike draws an analogy with the late British comedy actor Sid James, star of the 'Carry On' films and TV dramas in the 1960s and '70s. But whatever role he played, whatever he did, '*Sid was Sid*'.

> *'The great thing about all the different identities I have is that they are basically cartoons of myself. I'm always playing myself in different ways ... It's all about what I actually stand for. My philosophy is about having fun, about simplicity, about getting the point quickly, about being nice to people. It's a basic business philosophy, it informs everything I do, so I'm always consistent, not nice guy one moment and nasty the next.'*

 Mike

That authenticity is powerful, not having to put on pretences. You don't have to put on a suit that's not you or read from a script that isn't your voice or stand at the front of a lecture theatre if that's not your style. **It's about knowing your strengths, your style, your groove and sticking to it.**

You can PERSONALISE every element of your life when you become a Juggler. Even if you work for a huge company or a global corporation, whether you are a junior manager or a CEO, a freelancer or a start-up business, this is all about YOU.

12

Learning on the job

Juggling gives you the opportunity for low-risk experimentation – you are constantly learning. Try something. Anything. It doesn't need to be an all-or-nothing high-risk step; it can be part of a portfolio approach, adding something else small (or big) to the mix.

It doesn't matter if you screw up. Learn the lesson and move on.

It's stimulating and rewarding to try new stuff. And Planet Juggle creates the perfect ecosystem for that. It's good to learn and it's great to be curious. That drives not just juggling but also entrepreneurial spirit – you need to have curiosity to succeed.

Juggling takes you out of your comfort zone. Five years ago my business hadn't offered marketing services. Then I was asked to manage ad campaigns for a big brand, looking at media buying, dealing with designers. I'd never done it before. But once I'd spotted a business opportunity I just did it, learning on my way. Competing – and winning against – marketing businesses who'd done this all their lives.

Two years ago I had never written a book so again I learnt quickly about publishers, editors, proofs, royalties and advances. That's how I've always operated. Go beyond your comfort zone and core skill sets to juggle totally new disciplines and learn as you go.

Have the courage to take on new stuff to juggle, and relish the experience of expanding your horizons and also your know-how. Get involved in extra-curricular 'stuff'. A senior executive signed up for a 7-month blue-sky assignment. He had the opportunity to be part of a global task force doing really blue-sky stuff in Chicago for a huge brand. Big thinking, away from his core competencies. And he went for it and did it. Training his brain to think differently, working with different people, outside of the box (indeed outside of the box that the box is kept in!). A true Juggler, juggling not so much different tasks but ideas, concepts, vision.

Changes in the way we do business and the empowerment of technology in the workplace means each of us have had to embrace learning new stuff, regardless of our core roles:

'It is no longer acceptable ... for a CEO to have the secretary doing all the email or for

the marketing staff to not be able to write blog posts or for the IT director to not understand the customers' average tech abilities.'

 *Roxanne*

13

Staying hands-on

If you're bespoking your own work life, you can choose to stay hands-on. To do what you're good at and what you enjoy. So many managers and bosses find they miss the stuff that they were passionate about as they get promoted. A senior manager I was talking to recently said she was missing actually 'doing sales' rather than 'managing sales'. That's what she's great at, she doesn't like the management gig so much. A guy who runs a TV editing house said he was missing being a video editor, so now he's spending more time hands-on.

If that hands-on stuff drives you and that's what you're passionate about, there's no reason why you can't retain it as part of your juggle portfolio. You don't want to lose touch. If you are going to be a business leader, a consultant, advisor or even a blogger, you have to keep your hand in doing stuff. Otherwise what basis do you have for offering advice, what can you blog about if you are not a practitioner anymore? It's like an interview I heard with a rock band. They didn't want to spend too much time touring and away from reality, otherwise they would have no material for the next album.

14

Be an 'accidental success' – the importance of the non-plan!

The plan is – there is no plan.

Sure, part of being a Juggler is being that architect: redesigning your work life. But it's not having a grand strategic plan; more a flexible one that you are prepared to tear up when things need re-inventing (and they will need re-inventing). So you have to be flexible.

Andy Bird is Chairman of Walt Disney International. He works with Disney's business unit leaders around the world, tasked with coordinating and overseeing growth opportunities for the company. Andy describes himself as an 'accidental executive'; he never had a big plan, but advocates staying open-minded about opportunities:

> *'I don't have a game plan. I just want to do whatever I am asked to, do the best that I can, and I have got to have fun. If I don't have fun I have learned there is no point in doing it.'*

Andy Bird*

Andy's philosophy makes a lot of sense and it's obviously paid off as he's climbed to dizzy heights at the world's biggest entertainment corporation. So you have to keep it loose and stay open-minded.

Roxanne Darling feels she has made up her career as she went along but is also a firm believer in the importance of instinct.

> **'In hindsight, it sure feels like there have been some guiding forces in my life to make sense of the circuitous paths I have willingly taken. I do believe that when there is a strong desire for something, and it keeps showing up, then I am safe to explore it even though its value to me or relevance might not be apparent for many years.'**

 **Roxanne**

There isn't a career ladder for the Juggler (you try walking up a ladder juggling balls!); an economic crash or massive change could come from nowhere and the rungs are gone (actually, the whole damn ladder is gone).

Success evolves, it's organic, unknown. Survival relies on that flexibility. So you can't build a 5-year plan on where you or your business is going to be; you need to see what happens, be ready to be enterprising and be ready to juggle. Mike Southon also feels his career has been 'by accident' rather than part of a plan; success has been the result of being at the right place at the right time, sometimes doing things consciously, other times subconsciously.

And the most important tool to navigate you through your non-plan?

Instinct.

Go with your instinct every time and strive to be an 'Accidental Success'.

> **'I made it up. I only listen to my gut feelings and my gut talks to me often.'**

 Gary

15

The truth about multi-tasking

'Multi-tasking'. There's a business buzzword.

There are lots of myths about multi-tasking; it's not short-hand for not doing things well or them being done slop-pily. Multi-tasking doesn't mean checking your *BlackBerry* whilst listening to your client in a meeting; and it certainly doesn't mean driving home, talking on the phone and applying make-up (that's just rude and dangerous).

But it is having the mental dexterity to juggle multiple disciplines in the same mind space. Take journalism. Five years ago TV journalists just filed TV reports for fixed bulletins; now they write for the web, contribute to rolling news channels, and they blog. Some even film stories themselves. That's a lot to juggle: many styles, audiences and disciplines. But their message and their passion that unites it remain the same.

Sometimes, we don't realise how we much we juggle. Cheryl is a life coach and juggles a lot of other things besides. She made a list recently of all the balls she was juggling: Life coach; Entrepreneur; Businesswoman; Mother; Grandmother; Friend; Wife; Housekeeper;

Bookkeeper; Driver; Writer; Chef; Hostess; Wedding Planner; Gardener; Counsellor; Administrator. Like many of us, the challenge with those 17 is being across them in the same day or week. That is what true multi-tasking is.

Until Cheryl wrote these down she didn't realise the true scope of her breadth. But she knows her limits, which is why she took a much needed holiday recently.

Part Three

HOW TO DO IT ALL: JUGGLE TACTICS

When you juggle you might experience some challenges alongside the opportunities. How do you stay focused, how do you prioritise? How do you pull off living that multi-dimensional life?

Writing this book – right now – has been a live case study in juggling. I have been too busy with core business to clear the decks to focus just on writing so I have had to write the book alongside juggling two new projects, one ongoing project and my kids, with a schedule that mixes client meetings with writing trips.

And however good you are at it, juggling skills are something that you have to work on constantly.

> *'I'm always looking for how I can improve it. The thing about being a great Juggler is that you do have to work at it all the time in terms*

of your skills. Tiger Woods gets coached in
golf every day just to get that extra edge.'

 Mike

When you're keeping all those balls in the air, and everything's working well, then life feels great. But it can get
tough and it can be confusing.

How do you cope with the challenges?

There's no secret formula, no fixed rules you must follow,
no right and wrong when it comes to being an effective
Juggler.

But here's a bunch of tips that really work which can help
you get the most out of living the Juggle Life.

1

Manage time, all the time, every time

Here's the question.

How do you integrate work, family, fun, community and social commitment into your working day, week, life?

Success relies on how you deal with that precious commodity: TIME. On how you carve up your days, what you choose to do in your life, at work and in 'free time'. And in work, it's not about working longer hours at your desk; it's actually maximising the time you spend there.

Juggling time effectively is mainly about focus. Focus on the stuff you want to do. If you're going to integrate all that you're passionate about, forget the stuff that doesn't enrich you. So don't waste time on stuff you are not passionate about (life's too short).

And if you don't have the necessary bandwidth to handle something, say No.

'It's all about time management. I'm ruthless about my diary, the time I am spending, the people I am contacting, how

my networking is going. You need a brutal use of time because without that, time can fly past you. Ration your time if you can.'

 Mike

Rationing means maximising time; and sometimes that's recognising the value of brevity. If you can sum up that complex negotiation in a two-line email, then just do it. If you can distil that 145-page report down to 14 bullet points, great. If you can discuss and communicate a project status in a 15-minute meeting rather than a 2-hour one, do it.

Be adaptive with your approach to the working day. For instance, I don't *need* to work all day, every day. Some days I might start at 6am and end at 8pm; on others I start at 9.30am and end at 4pm. Some weekends I work. It all depends on what I am doing, what projects I have on. So you have to learn to be flexible. By all means, work 14-hour days when you need to; when you don't – don't. Make the most of your flexibility to do your own thing, to take time off and don't stay chained to your desk all day. And when you're getting stale, quit!

Think of scheduling tasks when you feel best able to perform them. Approach tasks intuitively. Schedule meetings to suit your culture and energy levels. Alter your rhythm and pace. If you know you need to free up time for creative thinking at the end of the month for that blue-sky project, then front-load your project workload so you sweat more up front and have more breathing space at the end. Much more efficient than the old way of burning the candle at both ends to deliver the report, project or product on time. The point of deadlines is that you can plan so you don't have to work a 20-hour day the day before something is due in. Try to schedule nothing-days where you have no meetings just to get stuff done.

Don't schedule tasks that require stacks of passion and energy for a Monday morning when you're not at your best. Manage your workload and to-do list to make the most of your talents, your time and your abilities.

'Being flexible enough to do tasks when your energy is aligned with them rather than on a fixed clock can lead to incredible improvements in efficiency and creativity. But that requires a sense of trust and personal responsibility for tracking the bigger picture and making sure key tasks are not overlooked indefinitely.'

 **Roxanne**

2

Segment your juggling

When you're juggling, your work life can get confusing. Case in point: this afternoon while I am trying to write this, I am also dealing with two other projects; that's three agendas at the same time. And it can be frustrating because I want to clear the decks and get stuck into one thing, not three things.

Although it's a fact of life that Jugglers have to be adept at dealing with multiple agendas simultaneously, try segmentation to make sure you stay focused on one thing at a time. Segment the working day for different bits. Because when I said juggling was about doing more than one thing at the same time, I didn't necessarily mean doing them all at 15:41 on a Monday, I meant in the same role, in the same day or week.

One approach to segmentation is to think how your job or role divides in simple disciplines. Is it Sales and Admin? Or Leadership and Project Management? Design and Client Liaison? Put simply, my job is 'Thinking' and 'Doing'; they are applicable to every project – they are ideas and delivery. Whilst they overlap constantly, to maximise productivity and performance I try and approach them differently.

The 'Doing' bit is probably 70%. Meetings, emails, sorting stuff out, talking, managing projects, implementing. For that I need a desk, a telephone, a laptop, a meeting room, my project files.

The 'Thinking' bit might only take 30%, sometimes even only 3% but THAT is where the value is. For that bit my tools are my brain, a pen and a pad, an airline ticket, a beer. Asking questions, coming up with answers. Strategising, formulating ideas for my business, ideas for my clients' businesses, ways to add value to projects, ideas for my next book. Some of this I try and do in a café, on a train, or in a plane. But you can't always contrive the climate for ideas generation; some results will just happen. During play time, in the shower, walking to the tube station.

Segment your schedule, your to-do list, your working week to maximise your productivity. If your energy levels are not at their best Monday mornings, don't attempt your big strategising then; save that for a Starbucks later in the week and get that sales report done instead. Work out where the 'value' is in what you do, and ensure you make the necessary investment in your time and your approach to get results.

3

Be a listophile

Nothing beats a good list for scheduling and reviewing tasks and priorities. It's a good way of managing the day-to-day, hour-to-hour.

So if you're a Juggler, love lists.

A list is great; it's a *brain dump* of all those things preoccupying you – whether it's choosing a wedding present for Peter and Joanna or preparing for that conference call. Both are important but keeping them in mind means they can conflict with all the other tasks your brain is contending with.

Keep on top of the details and lessen the mental load by writing everything down, whether ideas, thoughts, actions, deliverables. So simple, but often overlooked. Forget complicated project management tools or software, just an old fashioned list will do.

I was in a meeting last week; we were agreeing actions but one of the attendees didn't write anything down. And whatever his talents, I had no reassurance or confidence he'd do what we agreed. What happened if he went on to another meeting and forgot our action points?! In the end my colleague wrote it down for him. If you don't have agreed actions, then ambiguity, confusion and ultimately conflict can occur.

I'm such a listophile I sometimes have two lists per day. The one I wrote the day before for what I had scheduled for today; and the one I write as I go along doing project triage. It keeps changing and being added to. Then at around 5pm I cross-compare in case there's anything I really missed. Of course, my brain is constantly shifting gears, working out what's next. I'm not looking at the list to ask 'what's next?' but it's certainly my checklist for the day.

And having that checklist is important. I slipped off-list today. I was looking at a client website, followed a couple of links and was suddenly looking at a random blog, and my alter ego shouted 'what the f ... are you doing?' I was sucked into something with a very minimal chance of having that all-important return on investment. I gave myself a (figurative) slap and returned to the list.

Don't be too rigid (you're allowed to slip off sometimes) but a list is an efficient way of navigating your way through the chaos of a hectic juggle.

4

Make it a project

In your job you deal with lots of stuff. Not just meetings, emails, phone calls and tasks, but also goals, agendas, and disciplines.

Base your work portfolio on a project-centric basis. Each activity, whatever the discipline, is a project. Projects are united by having a client, a team, a timetable, objectives, a desired outcome. A start point, an end point.

So much of what we do now is project-shaped. Most businesses run their operations on a project basis. Workers reside in project teams, sometimes virtual, comprised of executives from different disciplines, countries and cultures, united with one objective. You come together on a project, whether one month, three months or a year, and then disband. Chances are, you'll juggle different projects, often overlapping ones, that will really stretch you as you struggle to find the capacity to handle them.

Juggling multiple activities that are seemingly open-ended – at the same time – could get draining but if you manage them by giving them a beginning and an end, and making them more finite and less random, then it's easier. Project-ise them. Give them a schedule, a deadline. And that pressure can help you achieve results. Where would we be without a deadline? Unfinished and undelivered. Or with products and projects that will never see the light of day.

I started writing this book on 17 June. I finished on 29 August. That's 73 days to write it. Yes, I had a few ideas before I started, but no more than a couple of hundred words, a couple of pages of notes. But from the start it was a clear project with objectives, deliverables and a delivery date. What made it easier was that sense of looming deadline. That sheer focus drove me.

So if some of the stuff you're juggling is too ambiguous or too unclear, try and rein it in. Box it in as a project.

5

Prioritise

Juggling multiple tasks and projects requires not just a clear head, but also an effective strategy. Running your day by a to-do list, knowing what things can wait, what to prioritise.

As you go through the day you need to carry out on-the-go triage as the day's events unfold. Triage is a great way of looking at things; it's a filter to evaluate and review progress, to define priorities.

Some days you'll feel like an air traffic controller, slotting tasks and projects into their place, repositioning them as the situation changes. Ready for change.

Roxanne Darling learnt from her partner Shane the importance of keeping a to-do list on a whiteboard, and finds it helpful working with him to refine the prioritisation process.

> *'One of the most valuable things I have learned is to be able to identify and sort tasks by the type of attention they require to be efficiently completed. I keep a whiteboard in my office and my home with the things on my To Do list, and I sort them by both amount of time needed for completion as well as the quality of time needed for completion.'*

 *Roxanne*

So you need to have clarity to focus and prioritise. That means standing back from things and making judgements of what to do now and next. And asking the question, 'what's mega urgent?'

> *'I go into the day looking at my calendar and knowing there are at least a couple bullet points I definitely want to accomplish. Meet-*

ings run long, things happen, so it's hard to always completely control the situation. Sometimes things have to get rescheduled and re-rescheduled but you have to prioritize.'

 Gary

Melanie Greene runs her own talent firm plus she's a Producer and Executive Producer of movies and TV shows: that's a lot to juggle. The biggest problem is finding the time to devote enough attention to each discipline on a day when they all need to be dealt with; to be there for all her clients at the same time.

'I'd like to tell you I had a magic formula which I rely on, but the bottom line is you deal with each on a priority basis. For example, if a client is leaving town to start a shoot the next day you make sure your staff have all the details of travel arrangements so that if anything goes wrong they can deal with it without having to involve me directly. (That) will free me up to deal with issues or meetings regarding other clients or to go to the set if I happen to be in production at the time. There is no doubt it's a delicate balancing act as you may have one or more client involved in a show you're producing and they obviously feel you're there for them.'

 Melanie

You'll get a good feel for what must be done now, and the stuff that can wait. The truth is knowing the difference and doing it in the right order.

6

Focus, focus, focus

When you have a lot to juggle, focusing on some tangibles can help your productivity and work efficiency.

Tangibles are goals, outcomes, actions, deliverables. Without focusing on these, time ticks by. A whole day can disappear.

You need some measuring stick for how you did today. Don't drift to random working, stay focused and make sure you're accountable to what you did in productivity; in ticking stuff off the to-do list or whiteboard.

Focus is also essential when you're struggling with *too* much to do; try blocking out time to devote to a task or a project like it was a meeting. It's a good way of allocating time, giving you that focus. Or shut down emails and phone calls so you can get on with something free of further distraction.

When you've got so much to do it can be easy to panic, thinking that you'll never do it. Or to put off doing stuff because you think it'll take ages to do. But if you focus clearly on one particular task or challenge at a time, it's remarkable what you can achieve in 30- or 60-minute chunks, allocating it a set time in which to attack and make some headway. So whether it's a project plan, budget or outlining a solution to a client challenge, just do it now; attempt it in a 30-minute session over a coffee or a 60-minute train ride.

Always go the extra mile to deliver a project or task but remember success is about delivery. Because there's no point in being a perfectionist if all that means is that you'll procrastinate and never actually finish something. That is why focusing – and meeting – a tangible goal is so important. What is the value of a perfectionist who doesn't ever finish a project because she isn't happy with it?

Juggling is about pragmatism – of aiming high but also delivering.

7

Get unplugged

Because we can – and do – work anywhere, the challenge is in switching off totally. It's absolutely crucial to be able to do that, to unplug your connections once in a while.

The trouble with technology like the *BlackBerry* is also its great benefit. As the ad says: *'connect to* **everything** *you love … all designed for the way you live today'*. That's what it trades on: it connects users with the life they lead; it integrates both business and personal. Sure I check emails on weekends and vacations, but it's when I choose to, I don't want it in my face 24/7. The whole point is that technology should help, not hinder; the *BlackBerry* is not the boss (nor is it your lover, so don't take it to bed with you). Get unplugged!

You have to find time and space to *dial it down*. To switch off, shut down and get real.

When Mike Southon travels overseas he tries to take his family with him; it gives him the opportunity to switch off after a speaking engagement and it's also a good excuse to disappear upstairs to his room.

'For me, family time is switch off time. All theatrical people know this – you're on stage /

you're off stage and you have different modes.
You learn how to control it. If you're 'on
stage' all the time you end up with a heart
attack. You switch in/you switch off.'

 Mike

But it's not just creating time for thinking or for the family; it's also the importance of creating ME time.

When you're flat out juggling, sometimes you need that quiet moment to give you sanity. A lie-in, a soak in the bath, a pint of Guinness by yourself, a seafront cycle, reading that novel for 10 minutes.

Roxanne Darling finds it difficult to turn off her business brain. Even on vacation she still wants to read her feeds and spots business opportunities frequently. Same with me. When Mike Southon goes on holiday he finds he can relax straight away without thinking of work, *'because nothing is that vital'*; but he still checks emails to filter them before his return.

When the schedule has been really manic, Kevin Roberts just unplugs for a few days and retreats to one of his homes. He doesn't take long holidays, preferring to take snatches of time here and there to switch off.

For Roxanne and her partner, it has been their company goal to be much more conscious of when they are 'on the client clock' compared to when they are off-duty. Their whiteboard system helps, as once the assigned tasks for the day are done, they feel better quitting.

> *'We are building the muscle to discern what is truly urgent and what can actually be added to the list. I also really let how hard we work weigh in and matter in our lives. One of the big plusses is being able to just stop and go to a movie in the afternoon if the day is crap and we are feeling burned out. It's easy enough to point to the hours we've undoubtedly put in, so the muscle is learning to take a break and realize if a client calls and we are unavailable for two hours, it is not the end of the world.'*

 **Roxanne**

So unplug yourself (and don't take your in-tray with you on holiday).

8

Bust your stress

Do you ever have one of those days when you wake up and think 'how on earth am I going to get everything done?' When you feel stressed, you know you have too much going on and lack the clarity to survive the chaos?

In my experience, there are two types of stress: good and bad. Stress when your life is rocking and rolling, you are juggling projects and play, busy and buzzy but life feels good. It's mad, but you feel on top of it. At the end of a busy day you feel stimulated by everything.

Then there's the other stress. That feeling in the pit of your stomach when you know you are under too much pressure. When that pressure feels unsustainable. And then – for the sake of your health and wellbeing – you know you have to do something. You need to heed the warning signs, temporarily allow yourself to drop a few of the balls, to focus on the real priorities.

Remind yourself that some of the stuff that gets chucked your way can just wait; don't drown in a sea of chaos. Sometimes you need to be tunnel-visioned to forget the 34 things on the to-do list and just worry about the 3 or 4 that *have* to get done before you go home tonight. Focus your energies there and you'll have a more productive working day.

I looked at my schedule a few days ahead of a holiday. And I was concerned that I wouldn't be able to do everything in time. I asked myself 'are all these meetings critical now?' Those that weren't, I cancelled. I'd created a false sense of chaos by putting too many meetings in at a time when I needed meeting-free days.

It's easy to get in a panic. Don't get in a cycle where you're stressed about being stressed! I know this guy who's always running around stressed; I feel stressed just watching him. When you break down his worries, they're hardly tangible. So whatever you do, don't create your own stress, by getting in a flap.

Here's a Stress-Busting checklist to deal with those panic moments:

1 Introduce a buffer to prevent you from getting too stressed out. Remove – or lessen – the pressure on your week, cancel that social engagement, dump your weekend plans to just chill and you can manage your stress levels.

2 Break the projects down to their basics. Consider what's important, what's not important and formulate a plan to get through the next 24 hours or whatever. And that will give you clarity and help you juggle.

3 Put things in perspective. Ask yourself, 'if this doesn't happen now, what's the worst thing that can happen?'

4 If you are suffering to-do list anxiety, set your alarm for 5am one day or spend a Saturday morning ploughing through actions and ticking them off with no interruptions. It's remarkable how much you can get done and also you can then approach Monday morning with clarity and a sense of being on top of stuff.

And if you are still struggling with everything and it's all getting too much, then:

→ STOP

→ PAUSE (that's the important bit)

→ REVIEW the to-do list

→ SHOUT 'Enough' and **raise the drawbridge**!

So, learn to know your stress levels and act. It's critical.

9

Getting connected

Fact: You Are Who You Know.

Success in business is so much about who you know; getting introductions and referrals, knowing the importance of word of mouth and connecting with people. And the more you do, the more connections you have.

If you do just one thing, your networking potential might be limited; whereas as a Juggler you have the opportunity to develop branches of different networks. Jugglers who trade on their black books and social/professional networks tend to have broader, more diverse networks.

Project managers in broad disciplines will know design-ers, technicians, accountants, sales guys, etc – they sit across everything rather than have a narrowly-focused network.

Such diversity of connections can enhance your life as well as your business prospects, hanging out with interesting people.

The more you juggle, the greater demands there are to keep in touch: clients, suppliers, team members, your network. Alongside those filters, develop a protocol for relationship management. If you're seeking to build a social or business network to try and build a community, use a blog to keep in touch, broadcasting to that com-munity. If you have the time – and the inclination – use *Twitter* to tweet to your followers on what you're up to. Two of our Jugglers have built big communities of fans and both Roxanne Darling and Kevin Roberts stay in touch with them on *Twitter*.

When you are so busy juggling, the simple stuff in rela-tionships can get overlooked. Stuff like regular communi-cation with a client, your boss or your team. So put in place some initiatives to schedule regular calls or meet-ings, even if it's just to say hi, to see how things are going.

Identify who your priority relationships are – clients, opinion formers, PAs of your targets, decision makers, people who sign off your expenses or authorise your invoice.

Keep those relationships maintained; they are the life-blood of your business.

10

Build effective relationships

Taking your contacts and building successful relationships with them can make the difference between a hassle-free life or a stressed-out one. Because relationships that are difficult can take a lot of time and energy to manage and troubleshoot. Not just in dealing with those people but also the mental energy wasted. Negative relationships are bad for your wellbeing; they can really sap your energy and positivity and, at worse, leave a bad vibe in the air. And none of the aforementioned is good for juggling.

A Juggler needs good karma to be effective.

So whether it's the guy you're dating, the boss you report to, the assistant you are hiring or the supplier you are appointing, make sure you strive for low-maintenance and reliable relationships. By low-maintenance I don't mean relationships that run themselves (because you still have to invest in low-maintenance ones), I mean reliable, safe-pair-of-hands people with a good attitude. That can make all the difference.

A difficult boss? I had one of those. It can make life unpleasant.

An accomplished take-care-of-it-all assistant or right-hand person? Absolutely essential. A supplier who gives you grief? I had one of those (and I thought 'I'm the client and *they're* giving *me* grief?'). A friend who is all take-take or me-me? That can get tedious.

So in your business and in your personal life avoid high-maintenance relationships, focus on people who yield value in whatever way. They're nice to deal with. They're straight, no bulls**t. Whether they are partners in your juggling or other people you spend parts of your life with, you'll find you can better maximise your time. You'll also be more able to segment those different bits of your life without the hassles bleeding through the edges from one part of your life to the other.

I was meeting some contacts for an after-work beer. I thought they'd be useful for some new business I was chasing; and also that they'd be good company for a couple of hours. But as I was sitting there with my pint, they were boring me with the banality of their conversation on some sports trivia. I thought, I could be at home reading my kids their bedtime story and then I realised something.

That in my carved-out life, I have an open-minded attitude to people and work and spend my days with a weird and wonderful mix of people. That means some days I've had a meeting with a peer at the House of Lords; other days I'll talk to a client on the other side of the world. But I realised in a flash that wasting an hour listening to these two muppets was not on my wish list. I made my excuses and left.

Don't hang out with timewasters; you'll get frustrated and it will get in the way of effective juggling.

In the cut and thrust of Hollywood, Melanie Greene has learnt the importance of being honourable in business and not wasting time with people who are not.

'Try to limit the amount of time you spend with people who you know to have been less than honourable in the past – that is, if you have to deal with them at all. Also always try to make sure you're not on anyone else's "dishonourable list". It means you never have to think twice about going back to do business anywhere and frees you up to think in a positive fashion about all the possibilities you have in front of you.'

 *Melanie*

In one her *Beach Walks* video podcasts, Roxanne talked on the theme of striking a balance between 'Give' and 'Take'.

She felt at that moment that she was giving more than she was taking and the imbalance needed to be restored. We might be so focused on giving – whether over-delivering on a project, doing something *pro bono* or helping out a sick relative – that we realise we've neglected the 'me' stuff. Be a good giver when you juggle but also learn to take too, and that means saying 'no' to stuff.

So from maximising that precious commodity of time, to a better quality of life, focus on relationships with the Nice Guys.

11

Ask yourself (often): 'where is the value in what you are doing right now?'

With lots to do, one of your biggest challenges in juggling is not so much what to do but, more importantly, what NOT to do. Choose to spend time on 'the wrong stuff' and you'll be wasting your time.

How can you ensure you focus on the Right Stuff? Apply value criteria in calculating what is a priority. Is the boss or client screaming for something? Is there a courier waiting outside for it? For everyday task prioritisation and 'Do I do this now?' stuff, you need to constantly ask this question:

'What or where is the value in what I am doing. Right now?'

Apply that question to dealing with that email, browsing that website, attending that meeting, seeing that supplier. You have to be ruthless with your time (and in 'play' too). That doesn't mean ruling out everything else; it just means make sure you know there's value in all you do. You can still take that 10 minutes to browse *FT.com* over a coffee or half-an-hour to go for that run. Because both of those have value (hey, take 10 minutes for a power nap, so long as you benefit from it!).

Ditto with tasks, meetings and projects. Value may not always be strictly about the bottom line, but other benefits. You have so many opportunities to evaluate, you have to – and in a flash – decide and prioritise. You have to make choices constantly.

We are all aware of the stuff that can take over our day. The stuff we don't really need to do, but get sucked into it. You need to try and eliminate distraction.

Stuff like random web surfing, browsing *Facebook* aimlessly, watching that 'Father Ted' clip on *YouTube*, anything that will give you cause to procrastinate what you are meant to be doing.

Asking the 'where is the value?' question is another way of looking at the much talked-about 80/20 rule: the principle that 20% of your efforts is responsible for 80% of your success. It's maximising that 20% and reducing wastage.

Also try asking yourself, '*is what I am doing now making a contribution to what I am all about*?' Sitting in this meeting, hanging out with this team, delivering this project, making this phone call, is this part of my DNA, is this who I am? And if you feel, 'this isn't me?' then act on it. Get out.

Use these criteria to make sure what you're doing now has a pay-off. That pay-off might not be today, might not be next week, but somewhere, where is the Return On Investment? It doesn't have to just be financial; it might be stimulation or fulfilment.

If there's no return, dump what you're doing.

12

Sell yourself!

Wherever you work, your personal brand is important.

You've got to be good at selling yourself. Not just at selling your company's products and services, but at selling You. Forget an aptitude for spreadsheets or being a genius at presentations; 'Personal Branding' is the latest must-have in any professional's toolkit. It's your whole business DNA – how you position yourself in the workplace, how you communicate your strengths and skills to people who count: clients, employers, target-makers.

Personal branding is so crucial, it can make all the difference in business success; it can dictate whether you get that bonus or turn your latest idea into a success. It's how you communicate your values, your business style and what makes you distinct. In everything you do, from first handshake with the client all the way through to sending them the contract, make sure you get noticed … and for the right reasons. You may have a job title that attempts to describe you but try to develop a personal brand that really defines you. Because 'Commercial Director', 'CEO', 'Designer', or 'Entrepreneur' is likely to be just the tip of the iceberg.

Grow a personal brand that reflects your whole DNA, from your business style through to your biography, business card and blog. Think of it as a set of business tools and business styles that sums up your essence. When you wear many hats, you may need to take that chameleon approach to self-branding. Today I'm a writer. Yesterday I was a video presenter. Tomorrow I'm an entrepreneur.

Whether you're sitting in an office in a big corporation or in a small start-up, the same principles apply. Remember, it's not just having a smart-looking CV when you are seeking your next job; it's about making sure that everything you do has your personal stamp on it: your style, your approach, your achievements.

No-one got anywhere by being mediocre, be great and then shout about it!

13

Be a one-man brand

When you're doing that selling, communicating your breadth to your organisation or marketplace, think like a big brand.

In the old days you had a CV, résumé, covering letter or positioning statement that you could tweak for different audiences: you could put the emphasis in one place for one job application; delete and embellish for others. But in the new digital space where social networking tools like blogs, *Twitter*, *Facebook* and *Linked In* showcase our talents, our identity is out there for all to see. That means you have to be authentic in your story.

This makes it so much easier to start a conversation and to build relationships – so if you want to get a meeting with a business guru in California or land in a CEO's in-box in Geneva, **nothing is impossible**. You just have to remember you are now 'searchable'; from your *Facebook* updates to your latest blog post – it's all out there. And in these outlets, work and play can get mixed up. Many people have 'professional' blogs; others start 'personal' ones. But the subject matter merges; a blog just becomes an expressive outlet for everything that's on your mind: personal, business, family, ideas, whatever. It's all mixed up.

Some of our Jugglers have created blogs and podcasts that showcase their talents, whilst building their brand and connecting with an audience. Mike Southon has a weekly column in *The Financial Times* newspaper, also online at *FT.com* and a weekly audio podcast. Gary Vaynerchuk and Roxanne Darling have web TV shows: *Wine Library TV* and *Beach Walks TV* are daily online video broadcasts with big followings.

Their video broadcasts instantly grow their sphere of operation and awareness. Roxanne of Hawaii suddenly becomes 'Rox of Beach Walks' fame, and Gary of New Jersey becomes 'Gary The Wine Guy'.

Gary really is a One-Man Brand. After having grown his father's wine business from $4m to $50m a year, he started *Wine Library TV*, a daily video blog that now reaches 80,000 regular viewers. He's had guest appearances on primetime TV shows and a bestselling book. All this from a 32-year-old son of Soviet immigrants that no-one in the States had heard of two years ago (and he hasn't even hit Europe yet!).

If you've seen Gary on *Wine Library TV*, you'll know that his success is about his passion; and that is an essential ingredient for any successful brand.

> *'It is impossible to transcribe a Gary Vaynerchuk perform-ance without capital letters and exclamation marks. He's an exclamation marks kind of guy. It is just the sort of opinionated, 13-to-the-dozen style that you need to stand*

*out in the blog soup of the internet. And stand out Vayner-
chuk does ...'*

Stephen Foley*

Gary is proof that anyone can build a personal brand;
anyone can harness the power of the internet and social
networking to become an expert. It's what Gary has billed,
'The Personal Brand Gold Rush'. You don't have to invest
much money, just a dedication and commitment to blog
or tweet. Start doing it and continue doing it. There are
no excuses for not bothering.

So be different, be remarkable and be your own brand.
You might lack the resources of a super-brand like Nike
or BMW, but even with a one-man personal brand, you
still have the power to make a difference.

14

Expect the unexpected

However robust your systems, your whiteboard, your to-do
list, your carefully planned week, s**t happens. So be flexible enough to embrace rapid change and go with the flow.

---

* 'The Grape Crusader', *The Independent*, 4 August 2008.

How many times have you spent the morning doing something *completely* different to what you planned to? Because you have to deal with stuff rapidly, to troubleshoot a project or turn a problem into an opportunity. To drop what you are doing and start something else.

It's 14:30 on a Thursday and everything I have done today was not – at any stage – on any to-do list. Two projects have thrown (considerable) curve balls at me. And I had to deal with them, to forget everything I was planning to do, and firefight a project. Check the customer was happy, chase a team member, take remedial action, do a bit of damage limitation. At the same time as managing a client's expectation on something else.

There was little I could have done to prepare for it. Apart from acknowledging that things go wrong and you have to deal with it (no choice).

You can try to take steps to get ready for whatever might be around the corner. Preparing for the unexpected means having some contingency. If you think tomorrow or next week's schedule is tight and there's no room for any slack, consider taking some pre-emptive action. Stay late at the office tonight to knock a few things off tomorrow's to-do list. Draft those emails while you have time now. Start writing that report while you have those ideas. Come in the office really early to get a head start. Because if you don't get ahead and something unexpected happens (as it will), you could be screwed.

Get ahead of the game and have the bandwidth to deal with firefighting a project or the unexpected. And if nothing unexpected happens, then you'll benefit from having more breathing space; you could even switch gears to take things easier.

15

Immerse yourself

Just because your role juggles lots of big projects doesn't mean you can neglect the details. Being across lots of things simultaneously – projects/departments/clients/parts of the business – means you need broad bandwidth.

Success is not always about completing the task as quickly as possible; consider the benefits of immersion where you soak up a project or a challenge over time. It's about living and breathing stuff.

If you attempt tasks too rapidly, you can miss the important stuff, whilst immersion over a longer period of time can mean you can really commit the time, energy and focus to drill-down, to pay attention to the details. To spot the detail that can really make a difference in a project's success.

Roxanne finds that some tasks can be done in the background before final immersion:

> *'Other things, like writing a client proposal, are best done when I can ruminate on it for many days or even weeks (in the background while I am exercising or reading my feeds). Then I like to carve out a block of several hours with no distractions to immerse myself and come out on the other side with a strong first draft.'*

 Roxanne

16

Be prepared to press delete

One of the most important questions you can ask, is **'should I, or shouldn't I?'** Sure, it's essential to know what's on your to-do list; but you also need to know what's on the not-to-do list. Don't waste time, be prepared to be ruthless. And one area that can really suck time is consuming information; especially in our electronic age, where so much knowledge is available and accessible online. It can be a huge distraction.

So you need some tactics. Sometimes you need to press delete on that email, hit 'unsubscribe' on that newsletter or chuck that magazine in the recycling bin. With unlimited resources online, it's tempting to spend too long consuming news about your industry or sector. Research can be a good use of time IF you can cap it, but be ruthless in your consumption.

I had a load of unplayed podcasts accumulating on my iPod. I thought, 'I should really listen to these; there might be something worth hearing.' But as I sat on the train I thought I'd rather listen to the new *Elbow* album than a bunch of business programmes. So I deleted the podcasts. And felt that burden lift! Big deal, what did I miss? Who knows (who cares?).

In consuming information I have trained myself to be good at scanning. What do I need to know? And then I move on. Because it's part of valuing time.

There's another filter you can experiment with – the power of instinct. Learn to consume and select by hunch. Use instinct as a tool because, unless you have a research assistant as a filter, it's the only way to deal with it without the risk of information overload, or worse – information anxiety. As you browse that book in Borders, is it worth picking up? As you click on the link through to a site that is either going to waste the next 10 minutes of your life or add enormous value, you have only one tool to decide. Instinct. Often, just by such a hunch (and nothing more scientific than that) I have found *the* article, *the* contact, *that* great nugget of inspiration, just like that. A hunch to click on that link, a hunch to buy the *FT* that day, a hunch to land on that life coach's website.

Don't overload yourself with data; be selective!

17

Dealing with those damn meetings

One of the biggest potential time wasters in every business, whether a three-person firm or a 50,000 corporation?
– 'Damn meetings'.

Maximising your time as a juggler means you need a good strategy for dealing with meetings. Many complain that meetings are a bad use of time. Managers and team leaders schedule meetings when an impromptu chat at a desk or a telephone call could have been more effective. Meetings with too many participants, or no clear objectives. But of course you can't eliminate meetings; you just need to manage them better.

Once I went to a meeting where the guy leading it said, 'this will take a day'!

A day-long meeting? (And it did take a day.)

How crap! What an utter waste of time. But don't do the other extreme. One colleague I worked with insisted on putting durations in minutes alongside agenda points for management meetings. Similarly flawed, if it says only '2 minutes' alongside 'Manager's Report' and it merits having 11 minutes, then you'd be accused of wasting meeting time if you talk for longer. But use your common sense. Keep it tight, keep a meeting focused. Agree actions there or in a follow-up email, the same day or next day. It's not about rushing things, it's about being rapid.

A good Juggler knows not to get lost in the bureaucracy of a meetings culture. It's a waste of time.

When you call a meeting, or get invited to one, ask:

! What is the purpose?

! Does it need a face-to-face meeting to get the desired result?

! Is it time-critical?

And if you go ahead with a meeting, ensure a tangible outcome every time.

18

Filter the crap!

Communication opens you, your role and your business to a wealth of opportunities. The more you juggle, the more your network of contacts snowballs. Great, but effective management of all this information and communication is absolutely essential.

You'll need to learn to filter approaches, enquiries and communications because the more successful you are, the more your profile grows, the more people will want to get hold of you.

It's not cutting off the lines of communication; it's more a need to establish a communication firewall to ease the pressure. It's a case of being selective. Until recently Mike Southon had removed his telephone number from his business card; he would rather be deluged with emails than voicemails. Gary Vaynerchuk now gets so many hundreds of emails a day, you get an auto response when you email him, explaining his protocol for handling mail and redirecting your enquiry where possible to others.

Have a good PA as a gatekeeper to process enquires. If you work for yourself and don't have an assistant, you can outsource to a virtual PA or digital concierge to run the admin side of your life. Consider technological solutions to screen emails and voicemails. Mike Southon is a fan of Spinvox, a technology that turns voicemails into emails/SMS text messages. He was getting so many telephone messages each day and he didn't know at a glance which ones were wanting to book him for a speaking engagement and which were general enquiries on entrepreneurship. Now he gets them turned into text, and manages all communications by the written word, whether they originated as emails or not. This is the best currency for him, a great way of 'time splicing', being able to filter out the urgent ones and deal with them.

Avoid communication overload. Implement filters to sort out the people you need to speak to from those you don't.

19

What's your script?

When we are introduced at networking events, meetings and dinner parties, the first question is usually the same:

'*What Do You* **Do**?'

I find it a bit tedious. The chameleon in me has a different answer depending on who's asking. Our Juggler Roxanne Darling sometimes answers it with 'When?'; instantly that gives a sense of the diversity of her days.

But the answer to the *'what do you do?'* question rarely defines the person. It's like that episode of *Frasier* when Roz starts dating a refuse collector. Everyone likes the new boyfriend but inevitably they all ask him, '… and what do you DO?' whereupon Roz quickly changes the conversation. He is totally comfortable telling people what he does but Roz is worried people will judge him and think less of him. But, of course, what he 'does' does not define him.

Mike Southon suggests we make our message relevant to the audience; he thinks a good sales person moulds themselves to what the customer is looking for. He takes the chameleon approach.

'I've got that standard salesman thing where I always ask them questions first. So I get a bit out of them first. Once I discoverer what they're in to, I can drop in 'oh, I play in a band' if they are interested in the showbiz stuff; if it's the public speaking or if it's a senior business person, first thing I say is that I've got my weekly column in **The Financial Times.***'*

 Mike

So alter your script accordingly.

My wife Zoë hates the question because her last job is not a good representation of her, so she developed a longer, more authentic statement:

> *'I've done a mix of stuff. I taught English in Tokyo, I worked for BridgeClimb in Sydney, I worked for an American technology start-up in London, and I set up my own business selling vinyl wall design. Now I'm busy looking after two small children.'*

Okay, it's a mouthful but it says a lot. It says Zoë likes travel, is enterprising, creative and an all-rounder. Some people judge others by their job titles. It's inevitable, but such a flawed criteria for communicating our unique talents and personality.

Gary V has a characteristically bullish view on this:

> **'I couldn't care less about answering that question to anyone. I know what I do and that's all I do, there's no sense in worrying about summarizing what I do.'**

 Gary

Sometimes success in business is about telling your story, rather than wearing a single label. And when you juggle – tell it like it is and ditch the labels.

20

Managing your identity

Wearing different hats can get confusing. Some people see you as one thing, others might see you as something completely different. But if you define your personal brand as YOU – beyond the job titles, beyond the labels – then that's much more authentic.

If we heard that the CEO Worldwide of Saatchi & Saatchi was also a lecturer in Business Studies and Chairman of USA Rugby we might wonder what on earth that has to do with being head of a global advertising agency; but as his brand is personified – 'Kevin Roberts' is the brand,* not 'Saatchi CEO' – then why can't this bloke called Kevin juggle nine different balls? He's defined by who he is, not a bunch of job titles.

Since you may be judged by perceptions (and the reality of your professional offering might be quite different from its perception), in a Juggle life your identity is really important. In all you do, you need to communicate your breadth. If you don't, people might think you are a one-trick pony and that will limit your potential. Be honest. Your work

---

* Even his professional website is called www.saatchikevin.com.

life should be a mirror of the real you; don't hide your talents – be your (full) self.

So if you only have a reputation for one thing, start shouting about the other bits. Communicate your personality. What's the first thing I do when I check out a business online? I go and look at the People bit of the company's website – who works there, who runs them, what they've done – and that helps define the personality bit of their brand. Some business websites do a good job of communicating personality. The UK ad agency Mother had a website where the profile of its staff mentioned everything but their professional identity: their eye colour, their nickname, stuff they like, passions and quirks.

This new media space offers fantastic opportunities to communicate our multi-dimensional selves and to be really transparent:

'I think that every person is multi-dimensional and has enormous things they are good at and many different interests and I think that the best way to communicate in this new social era is to talk about all of them, don't hide anything ... I think people will always embrace 'real' and 'authenticity' and I think the more things you talk about that you are passionate about, I think the more people are going to get to know who you are. So please

don't fear being multi-dimensional. Expand
what you are talking about.'

 Gary

I just updated my blog and it excited me. I felt, 'This is
Me'; this is a total snapshot of who I am, every part of
me. In one single destination. Whoever lands on this web
page now will 'get me'. And that is a powerful thing to
communicate.

So use your biog on the company website to stand out
from the crowd. Use whatever platforms you have at your
disposal to TELL THE STORY: whether *Facebook*, *Twitter*,
your blog, show your passions. Mix it all up together. Tell
it like it is. Work. Play. Family. Hobbies. Whatever.

21

What to do with your quirky side?

If Juggling is about the real you, what do you do about
the quirky side?

!   On the surface you are a straight-laced accountant but
then you are a children's entertainer at weekends?

! You're a serious CEO but crazy about cute cats?

! You're a hot-shot M&A lawyer but write erotica on the side?

Me? I've co-devised a kid's book (but I don't talk about it much).

Wherever possible, don't hide it.

Every Juggler is unique, a bespoke portfolio of loves, skills and projects that are the make-up of their identity. That's the joy of being a Juggler: no requirement to conform, you can freestyle your life. So optimise what makes you distinctive.

Make sure your brand communicates that wacky side. If you run your own small business, make sure your offering, philosophy, website reflect that diversity and celebrate those differences.

Mike Southon is a heavyweight business speaker but plays in a band, *Mike Fab-Gere & the Permissive Society*, where he dresses up in an 'afro' wig and 1970s clothes and entertains clients on stage. It's part of who he is; it's part of the Mike Southon story. He loves music and he loves to have fun. Some clients get Mike Fab-Gere, others don't. Sometimes he'll do an event and do 'Serious Mike' throughout the day and 'Crazy Mike' in the wig at night, and the audience don't realise it's the same guy!

Either way, Mike has fun with his alter ego, and he gets paid for it. A multi-dimensional identity doing loads of different stuff and juggling various balls is what makes you distinctive. It's what your passion and *raison d'être* is all about. So don't even think about diluting it.

> *'Most people do not expect male assistant professors at a prestigious business school to wear black leather trousers, shave their heads, do gigs, listen to* The Prodigy *CDs, take half a year of paternity leave and so on. But we do, because we feel like it.'*

Kjell Nordstrom and Jonas Ridderstrale, Funky Business*

So get funky! Ask yourself, what would people love to know about you? If you could unleash the Real You what would it be? Open up and reveal your passions. And strive to be different. It can be very powerful.

---

* *Funky Business* by Kjell Nordstrom and Jonas Ridderstrale (*Financial Times*/Prentice Hall 2001).

22

Create your juggle jungle!

When you are juggling you need to create your very own eco-system, an environment with all the ingredients to support your efforts. Think of it as your *Juggle Jungle*!

You'll need ingredients like:

! A place (or places) to work that stimulates you.

! Places to think that inspire you.

! A supportive team, boss or assistant to help you.

! A supportive partner at home to lean on.

! Tenacity and resilience to be a success.

! A set of guidelines and principles to make sure you survive.

Having a supportive partner and family should not be overlooked. When you're manic, stability in your family and friends is crucial. This juggling game has a lot of challenges; mentally, you may feel all over the place as you struggle to tie it all together. An understanding husband, wife or partner who understands the challenges as well as the benefits of juggling can make all the difference. A partner who isn't going to protest when you say you need to work on a Saturday and they have to look after the kids.

And it's not just having an understanding partner or a genius PA or supportive team around you. It's having other tools to deal with those inevitable challenges that get thrown your way.

Develop a strict set of guidelines to deal with a manic schedule. I spoke to a busy executive who spends a lot of his time flying around the world. Through all he does he has some strict guidelines. He always tries to be home for the weekend, wherever he is in the world; he makes sure he gets enough sleep; and on his overseas trips he makes sure he doesn't skip meals and that he drinks lots of water. That may sound trivial but that regime can make a real difference when you're juggling. You may not be able to control airline timetables, bad weather and jet lag, so make sure you look after those things you can control.

Kevin Roberts has similar tactics; he creates an eco-system to give him that constant in a busy travel schedule, one that relies on great logistics and familiarity. He stays in the same hotels, takes the same airlines, sits in the same seats, has the same drivers, and a team of four assistants to organise everything.

We don't all have assistants; some of us don't have options for delegation. But even having a mate who will support you, help out or even just be understanding when you can't come to the pub for your usual Friday night beer; all that is invaluable.

Go plant your seeds for the Juggle Jungle!

23

Having places to do and be

Different places can help reflect the multi-dimensional you. You'll have your office, perhaps a workspace at home, favourite coffee shops where you do certain things and weekend places where you do others, a summerhouse at the end of the garden or a park bench.

When the coffee shop trend started up in the early 1990s they were trying to create what was billed a 'Third Place' between work and home, a space that mixed social with work. Well forget Third Place, more like 33 places. We are nomadic, working from airplanes, trains, wherever. There are no rules and no walls to where and how we work.

In the week I met him in Paris, Kevin Roberts' schedule was taking in Mexico, Miami, Peru and Brussels. With his offices in New York and New Zealand and homes in New York, New Zealand, St Tropez and Grasmere in the UK, this guy travels a heck of a lot. All contribute – in different ways – to making him an effective Juggler.

> *'All of them connect past, present and future. All of them have work, play, friendship and family relevance. All of them are perfectly set up for me to be effective and efficient in terms of work. The different bases help me juggle because all of them are themed differently and are typical of their regions. They all have meaning and all serve to inspire me. New York is an abstract art-driven Tribeca loft, Grasmere is a typical Lakeland cottage in National Park land. St Tropez is a Provence villa, and New Zealand is an environmentally friendly sports complex.'*

 Kevin

But you don't need to have four homes around the world to be a good Juggler. You can create your own diversity through different spaces that energise and stimulate you, whether hotel rooms, cafés, workspaces or open spaces. These can reflect different sides of your personality. I have a mix of 'zones' – client offices, member clubs, coffee shops, workspaces – each of which has played its own contribution as a space to juggle. Spaces for meeting, for thinking, for writing, for problem solving, each with their own source of inspiration.

24

Go on an inspiration jaunt

For centuries, artists have travelled the world in search of new landscapes and vistas for inspiration. Those journeys and fresh perspectives have fuelled great results. So why not apply the artists' approach to business executives?

Consider the value of mini breaks and timeouts as 'Inspiration Jaunts'; as an investment in both your intellectual capital and wellbeing.

Time off or time out is not just about relaxing or being on holiday. It's a recharge of your battery and a necessary mental work-out.

Think of the value of holidays in getting that fresh perspective. Then try and create mini holidays in your life that stimulate the brain and offer wellbeing, inspiration or stimulation. Lie in the park on a sunny day at lunchtime, go on a journey. If it's not feasible to take a holiday, take an afternoon off or a long weekend and see the benefits. 24 hours could be as valuable as one week.

These Inspiration Jaunts provide great value. Stuff like:

! New experiences and new places to inspire.

! Isolation to focus on something.

! Liberation from the 9–5.

! It can feel like 'a treat'.

! Or just provide some relaxation.

I take short breaks to inspire a project, a new venture or my writing. They are my oxygen for fuelling my next idea. I always find journeys so productive for ideas generation. That first beer on a flight or the first coffee on Eurostar gets me fired up to be really productive in my notepad or laptop. It can be tough carving out that time amongst other projects to release the time; but it's always worth it. It always pays off.

To start writing this book, I created an Inspiration Jaunt to the South of France.* Just three days, but the journey, the isolation, the buzz, the different environment, away from emails and distractions really fired me up. With the focus of that trip, the themes for this book came together. In the sunshine, at a café I scribbled my ideas.

A friend called to ask how 'my holiday' was going. 'I'm not on holiday,' I replied. But then I didn't *look* like I was at work either (since I 'am my office', I'd taken it with me

---

* Three days in Nice in June. It was a tough gig but someone had to do it. …

anyway). I was working and playing together, seamlessly. I might have been sitting there with a glass of wine in the sunshine, but it's an investment in my intellectual capital, in my next big idea. And that's a bloody important investment. The pressure to deliver helped me get results; to return from the Inspiration Jaunt with an empty notepad was just not an option.

Good ideas are at the heart of every successful business. So you need to be a good ideas person. Be aware of what stimulates and inspires you. You're unlikely to have good ideas working at your desk, so get out there. You need to play, to reflect, to stand back from the day to day. So go to the pub, go the park, go on a trip somewhere.

My destinations to help write this book had different influences, just like the value of Kevin Roberts' different homes and offices for his inspiration. Nice in the South of France was for the 'nice' bits, a good place for the project gestation, somewhere to scribble thoughts in the sunshine and develop ideas. That was my Mediterranean retreat. My North European equivalent in Amsterdam where I finished it off? A hotel room like a writer's garret up a steep staircase. A wooden floored big room with a glass desk and a sofa. That was for the head-down, polish-the-project-off bit.

Kevin reminds us that '*inspiration out is a big result of inspiration in*' (i.e. you want to *have* some inspiring ideas? Go *get* inspired!) So, like me, he's a big fan of taking random trips away. Whether you have a big deal to consider, a big idea to devise or you just need a recharge, take an Inspiration Jaunt.

25

Give yourself a treat and the importance of 660 seconds

When you're working flat out, give yourself a treat, however small in time or value.

I was working at home today writing this book and dealing with some projects. It's early evening and I fancied a beer so I went down to the kitchen to get one. My two-year-old son intercepted me and wanted me to play football with him in the garden before bedtime. I obliged. We had great fun, kicking the ball around in the late sun. Now I'm back at my desk in work mode and diving into some emails. iTunes is still playing on shuffle and tells me 11 minutes has elapsed since I was last at my desk.

11 minutes.
Just 660 seconds.
Not long.

Enough time to go to your workspace kitchen and get a coffee, or if you're a smoker to go down to the lobby and huddle on the pavement with a cigarette. Or enough time to get lost in a random website. But 11 minutes with my boy was – literally – the highlight of my day. No debate.

Never underestimate the power of small nuggets of reward when you are juggling. They are so very important. You need a pay-off if the stuff you're doing today/next week is tough or dull (or both).

So give yourself a reward; something you want to do, or that will give you a 'feel good' factor. Stuff like:

! A lunch out, not at your desk.

! The gym or a run.

! Write a blog post.

! A bar of chocolate this afternoon when your energy levels are flagging.

! Look forward to that first beer of the day when you finish work.

! Treat yourself to a take-away dinner tonight.

! A quick game of football with your son.

! Sex!

It may sound silly, but that goal of a reward can really motivate you when your energy levels or morale are flagging. It will inspire great results.

Create a 660-second break in your day.

26

Don't be a workaholic

For most of us, to be successful you have to work hard. But that doesn't mean you need to be a workaholic.

If we work too hard, it's crap. Crap for us, our co-workers and our families. No-one really benefits. Our projects don't, our clients don't and our productivity certainly doesn't.

Set some limits. Know when it's time to switch off/stand back. Otherwise you'll jeopardise the things that REALLY matter. Stuff like:

! Your quality of life.

! Your friends and family.

! Your health and wellbeing.

! Your ability to relax.

I read a profile of an executive who worked flat out in a senior role, from first thing in the morning through to 10pm. He had two children and another two from an earlier marriage. He has a full life as a successful executive but rarely sees his children. What's the point of that?

Make sure that you punctuate your schedule with down-time. Develop some personal rules, find time for play time or exercise, try and switch off on a flight or a business trip and turn off the mobile and the *BlackBerry* at night.

Stick to those rules when you can and know the benefits of switching off from the to-do list to do some thinking or just to get unplugged.

Melanie Greene has a hectic schedule to juggle and often finds herself at screenings and networking in the evenings. But she enjoys that side of things, so it doesn't seem too much like work.

> *'I've always been highly motivated and I enjoy working and social situations and this business has a lot of those – thankfully I don't mind that aspect within reason.'*

 *Melanie*

There's a fine line between working hard and working too hard. Because the more projects you're across, the more you need space to breathe.

Most of us have got used to working in an 'Always-on, Never-off' culture. Maybe we need to take some cues from our continental European friends. French and Spanish execs work hard but take lunch seriously – it's not just a sandwich balanced on the in-tray. A friend of mine in France takes lunch at a restaurant every day. It's part of the culture, it's more civilised and gives him that pause in the day.

Ultimately you need to maximise time so you don't sweat so much. So just when you think you are too damn busy juggling to do anything other than have a sandwich over your desk, maybe go out and sit down for 40 minutes. The world won't collapse and you may get a new perspective, feeling better fuelled to deal with your juggling for the rest of the day.

27

Remember to come up for air

You're busy. Leaping from one meeting to another, juggling different agendas. Then you have a call to make; you switch off emails while you write that report your boss is waiting for. The day is destined to be back-to-back priorities with no time for anything else.

Four words of advice:

Come up for air.

Remember to resurface so you can:

! Take a breath and glance at your to-do list.

! Suddenly remember, 'oops, I said I'd call the client back by 4', or 'oops, I forgot the card for our wedding anniversary tomorrow'.

! Have a breath of fresh air (literally).

! Make a cup of tea.

! Take time out for that 'eureka' idea.

The trouble is that so many of us get embedded in our working lives, we throw ourselves headlong into our jobs, giving that inevitable 110%. And the better we do, the more stuff we get thrown at us. New responsibilities, new projects, new divisions to run, new people to manage. Which means we become very adept at running stuff, but not so good at thinking about stuff.

And in order to get more out of life, you need to be good at the ideas bit. Coming up for air will free yourself from clutter and give you the clarity to be open to new opportunities that you may have missed if you had your head down in a panic.

Remember, you're not going to have those 'eureka' moments at your desk. Go for a coffee, go for a walk, go on an Inspiration Jaunt, do anything and everything **other** than sit at your desk.

Coming up for air is really valuable on days when you are manic, because it's the last thing you think you have time for as you are so pushed for time. But if you don't surface for air and stand back for a minute there'll be stacks of stuff you'll overlook or just plain forget.

So, whether it's for that 'oops' moment, to get a fresh perspective or to take five minutes out, get some air.

28

Be fit to juggle!

To be a good Juggler you need to be physically and mentally healthy. All the obvious stuff. No hangovers. Drink plenty of water, have plenty of sleep. And easy on the espressos (note to self).

It's no coincidence that our successful Jugglers try to punctuate their daily lives with exercise. We all need to get the endorphins going, to stretch the body whilst stretching the mind. Kevin Roberts starts the day – every day – with an hour of cardio, whether tennis, gym or cycle. Each of his homes is geared up for 'maximum work efficiency and for health'. He has gyms in all four, tennis courts in two of them, and bikes in all four.*

Mike Southon doesn't usually find time for play in his working week so he makes sure he schedules exercise at the weekend, running around Hampstead Heath every Saturday.

But don't think you need to be eligible for *Ironman of Europe* to take exercise seriously. The small stuff can make

---

* Is there a correlation between Kevin Roberts' success and the fact that he has a gym and a bicycle in every one of his homes?!

a difference too. It's amazing what a 20-minute run can do for the soul, let alone the lungs. Roxanne Darling takes a daily morning swim that sets a base that lasts the entire day.

Exercise can be that tonic or just provide a healthy punctuation mark in a busy day. Trevor is a successful coach and consultant. When he can, when he's working at home he and his wife (who's also his business partner) go for a daily midday walk with the dogs, and a run when they can.

You'll also need some sleep (something my 11-month-old son Dylan likes to jeopardise). Kevin ensures he sleeps on every flight he takes as he knows we need a reservoir of sleep to dip into, to support our juggling.

Practising yoga can also be a great leveller for the stress of the day. Melanie Greene has been running her success-ful Hollywood talent management firm for 25 years; it can be an all-consuming role with high-profile clients, unfore-seen challenges and a very demanding work schedule. Yoga's her release.

'I take a yoga class three times a week and I try to run as well and I find that helps me keep my head clear. I'm not saying that there aren't days when it isn't difficult but I'm proud to say I've kept it going for over 25 years now so I guess somewhere in my system

there now exists a mechanism to cope with whatever is thrown at me.'

Melanie

So don't think this isn't important; it can make a huge difference to wellbeing, attitude and productivity.

29

What turns you on?

What's your currency of stimulation? What gets you going?

Maximising your juggling abilities; inspiring a solution to your latest challenge; or getting that required motivation – know what drives you.

Is it an early morning swim? A run? The view from your window? You need to know what it takes to get the most out of work and life.

If walking to the top of a mountain drives your productivity and happiness, act on it. Go and find a mountain!

If you're best at 06:00 or best at 22:00, act on it – start early or work late.

Be self-aware of your stimuli and, wherever possible, build them into your working practices, into your lifestyle. And REDESIGN YOUR WORKLIFE accordingly. If you're crap before 10:00 have a policy of not doing breakfast meetings. If you're best after a gym session or a cycle, do it. Ditto your daily espresso, tulips on your desk, the *Foo Fighters* on your iPod, your lunch break in the park, whatever IT is that turns you on.

Kevin Roberts' stimuli are different homes with different vibes; also his 12,000 tracks on the iPod, the four books he reads at any one time. For me it's the change of perspective and focus of a journey somewhere; for my editor, Sarah, it's fresh flowers, a clean and clear environment.

If you don't feel in the right zone, try and break it. Switch projects. Go for a run, for a coffee, put the kettle on. Walk away from your desk. Go and read a book for half an hour.

Pause. And then wait for the results. And watch that inspiration flow; your energy levels lift or the eureka moment realised.

30

Having a team

Perhaps it's no coincidence that our Jugglers who either operate in big corporations or who are more senior tend to have a better time juggling. Even though the scope of their decisions and projects is massive, they have teams of people to delegate to and support them. And whilst that may bring challenges in management, in pure juggling terms it means they can focus on the big stuff.

A Juggler needs a great support infrastructure to manage appointments, schedules and clients.

'The most important element is that I have great people and terrific logistics. Trudy has been with Saatchi & Saatchi 25 years and heads up a team of three assistants in New York, New Zealand, and the UK. Trudy coordinates my work and personal life as a full-time partner. If you've watched MASH, she is Radar O'Reilly. She knows Saatchi, she knows our people, she knows our clients, she knows our priorities and she knows my rhythm. She's proactive and forward thinking. She's also an expert Juggler handling her commitments, her

family, and some outside community com-mitments superbly.'

 Kevin

If you have fewer people around for support, then it can be more difficult to juggle. Because you have to mix the huge with the tiny, you have to do everything.

This applies to my own business where I have a virtual team of co-workers on each project but lack the reach-out-and-touch colleagues or assistants who can really make the difference when you're up against it.

A good Juggler needs an effective team, as his or her troops. It will make a difference on those days when you are really up against it.

31

Delegate and outsource

One way to maximise time and concentrate on important stuff is to focus on being truly excellent/outstanding at **what you're good at and what you love**. Stuff you're no good at? Forget it. Delegate or outsource those travel arrangements, that tax return, whatever. Why try and master something you don't enjoy?

> *'It all starts with knowing when you are at your best and playing there all the time. I focus on those things I'm good at and try to get world class at them. The stuff I can't do I ask others to handle and choose people who are brilliant at it, significantly better than me at least. None of us is as good as all of us and I make sure that I have a bunch of inspired people around me who are all experts in their fields.'*

 Kevin

Melanie Greene acknowledges that, however much she delegates, it's different when it's your business. Because you probably underestimate the know-how you take for granted; that's stored away in your subconscious. Also, when it's *your* business, you want to know how it's doing, even when you're not there.

> *'In reality when it's your own business no matter who your staff are or how good they are no-one is as passionate about it as you are. Also, because the management side of the business involves so much knowledge that you store in your head, there's only a certain amount of delegation that you can do*

so you do tend to check in more, even when you're on holiday.'

 *Melanie*

In all you're doing, when there are options for delegating, ask yourself: 'is this task the best use of my time?'; 'Am I enjoying it?'; 'Could I be doing something more productive instead?' And if the answers are no, no, yes then do something about it! It's like I'm not going to try and master web design because 1) I don't want to and 2) it's more efficient to outsource.

These days there's so much pressure to be a tri-athlete, to master Mandarin or go to the gym, you have to make choices. **Stick to your passions and ditch the rest** is not a bad mantra. Not only does it allow you to focus on your strengths; it frees you up to juggle the other things in life you need time for.

Success is knowing what drives you and listening to your heart, so outsource and delegate what you can and you'll be liberated for what you want to do. That's how Kevin Roberts pulls it off!

'We have a stripped down, simplified structure and business process which allows me to be hands-on in the areas that matter, and hands-off in the areas that other people do better than me. This allows me time to advise my wife, Rowena, on her $6MM busi-

ness in New Zealand, to be Chairman of USA Rugby (a passion of mine), to be the CEO in Residence at Cambridge University, and to write.'

 Kevin

32

Hire a digital assistant

If you're in a role or organisation where it's just you with no-one to delegate to, you need to develop some tools to help manage yourself.

You might not have a real assistant, so consider technology as your very own digital assistant. Technology can make a difference in making your work life just a little bit easier. Use tools at your disposal to manage your information flow; for example, have *Google Alerts* to surf the web for you, *Google Reader* to collate your blog and website content, *Outlook* to invite meeting attendants. Download podcasts to your iPod and re-engineer the way you consume content to make it revolve around you, not the other way round.

Jenny works in publishing and, with no-one to delegate to, she needs to ensure her tasks and information flow are well planned. She sets herself reminders to go off in her Calendar and has created different folders within *Outlook* to process emails.

> *'I have folders like: "To Do" which keeps my inbox clear as I just move tasks into this folder; "By End of Day" for urgent tasks that need to be completed; "Awaiting Responses" which I check regularly to see if anyone needs chasing for a response, etc. All of this helps to make sure that nothing is forgotten about and is dealt with when necessary.'*

Jenny Ng, Assistant Editor

And as someone who's on the receiving end of Jenny's planning, I can tell you – it works. She's most definitely that *safe pair of hands*.

If you get it right, you can save time, work more effectively and even liberate yourself to spend less time at your desk.

33

Lose the guilt!

Guilt can be a real issue for us Jugglers.

And it goes two ways. Don't feel guilty working on a Saturday or Sunday when the family would rather have your time, because once you've done that report or dealt with those emails you'll be able to feel relaxed and give them more. There's nothing worse than a preoccupied partner, trying to play or relax but failing badly because they have too many work worries. So if it's that bad or that pressing, just get it done now and then you can breathe a sigh of relief. The *quid pro quo* of your family having you on a Friday afternoon might be that you have to do some work Saturday afternoon.

Similarly don't feel guilty NOT working weekends if you have a lot on. It's knowing when it's time to switch off or quit for the day. So don't feel guilty about seeing a movie or going for a swim during the day.

Roxanne Darling says that with the explosion in online content and the success of her *Beach Walks TV* video blog, there is tremendous pressure to be constantly interacting with her audience. As well as producing and presenting a sometimes-daily *Beach Walks*, she has a social networking site 'The Reef', plus there's the day job: a small business to run. She's in demand! It's tough to carve out that time every day to do *Beach Walks*. But success is deciding what is important and what is not.

> *'The real core of this is to appreciate my own energy and find a way to share that energy with the people I truly treasure the most. And we do manage to cut out on the spur when we both feel the need to refresh at a movie or walk on the beach (without camera). It doesn't happen very often, however, when it does, I no longer feel guilty! Our ability to work hard and produce both for our clients, our community and ourselves, is well-documented, internally and externally.'*

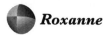 **Roxanne**

34

Sorting out the home life

I had lunch in a bar the other day and the couple at the next table were trying to organise their domestic life. I couldn't help but listen. She sounded stressed; going through her diary explaining what they were doing the next few weekends, and telling him when she was out: a leaving drink at her office one evening, going to see a play with a friend another. She was concerned about keeping their apartment clean and doing the laundry. I felt sorry for them; I was feeling pressured just eavesdropping!

If work life is too busy juggling, switch down a couple of gears for the social life. Try a very complicated work life and a less complicated social life. If you're blocked out every evening Monday to Friday then you need to create time out. When I had a very demanding day job and was out every single night with friends or colleagues, I knew I had to put the breaks on sometimes and have a 'buffer' evening, when I cancelled whatever it was I was meant to be doing and had a night in. My mind, body and business needed it.

Don't view your home life as your second job and don't treat the relationship with your life partner like you do with your co-workers. As it is, work is where you might have less choice than your home life, so make some choices in the social. The social is meant to be fun, so don't waste time on meeting friends you don't really want to see or going to a wedding of some tenuous friend who means little to you.

Make choices, be ruthless and don't over commit. And if your partner needs to make an appointment to see you or if your kids wonder who Mummy and Daddy are because you're never there, you're doing something wrong. Shift your juggling and get your priorities right.

35

Set the alarm clock!

Some people are cynical about the life of a Juggler. How on earth does he have time for a run in the morning, how can she start every Monday morning at the gym, how come he's sitting having a coffee this afternoon? How does she have time to write a blog or write that book?!

Enjoying juggling and benefiting from flexibility is about good planning to make sure your lifestyle is geared to your individual needs. If you need to go training for triathlons, you carve out a lifestyle that gives you that. If you want to juggle the job with looking after the kids, ditto.

On seeing my blog, one friend said she was surprised that I had time to contribute posts to it. It's actually just about focus and priority. To have the discipline and to make the commitment to blogging need not take much time, it's a matter of minutes. It's about priorities. I look at websites and blogs and see the same contributors making long, well-thought-out comments every single day. And I ask myself, 'how on earth do they have time?' but they have made that a priority and make necessary sacrifices to do it, such as blogging rather than reading a book or going to bed an hour earlier. And the same applies to any other priority.

Good Jugglers need to make the day really productive; taking that 24 hours of a blank canvas and maximising its potential.

Gary V is a busy man. How does he do so much? According to *Wired* magazine* the guy hardly sleeps. *Wired* broke down Gary's day on 29 April 2008 and reported he spent just 4 hours 24 minutes sleeping and just 24 minutes eating. Which leaves stacks of time for everything else; an incredible 12 hours 12 minutes responding to emails. This evidence is cited as how he has built such a loyal following – by dealing with and responding to his fans of *Vayniacs*. There's a clear correlation between Gary's success and his schedule – he doesn't get much sleep!

So here's some simple advice for people who want to have time for more stuff, but struggle for time:

Try getting up earlier! (Or going to bed later.)

---

*   *Wired*, August 2008.

It works.

It makes a big difference, having more hours in the day to carve up. It sometimes really is that simple.

36

Think: what's next?

When you're head-down and juggling, it's easy to have your head so far down it's stuck in the sand. But don't become so preoccupied with the present that you forget the future.

And this is an easy mistake for many Jugglers. Sure, it's a good coping strategy to take things day by day, but what about when that project pipeline comes to an end, what happens when you've exhausted all your current leads? What are you going to say when your boss asks what developments you have planned for the next quarter? Whatever your job, show your strengths by thinking ahead.

One way to segment your approach to deal with the future – think 'Maintenance' and think 'Development'. You have to juggle the maintenance of your role and your responsibilities (that's the day-to-day) but don't neglect development: what next for your role, projects, department, business (that's the future bit)? Too many people say they are too busy managing delivery of projects to have time to think about business development or brainstorming the future.

But that's the whole point of juggling – you have to do both together (of course).

Do you know 'what's next?' If you don't know, have a think about it …

Part Four

HOW TO HAVE IT ALL: JUGGLE LIFESTYLE

Do you believe it's possible to be successful in business and not sacrifice your life?

Of course, that is the objective.

Don't think that if you are going to have a great job or run a successful business that you can't also have a great personal life. Because you can.

The goal is in having both that sustainable economic model and the sustainable lifestyle model. What the heck does that mean?! Make enough money and be happy! The key is very simple: do stuff you enjoy. Be passionate about it (and don't do the stuff you don't enjoy).

Once you've redesigned your work life, full of stuff you're good at, and stuff you want to do, you can have it all.

What's the best thing about my life? I'm in control of what I do. I choose what to do. The 'Work Ian' is the 'Real Ian'. I'm at one. And it's not just being The Real You, it's also being The Best You, The Happiest You. All options are achievable.

If you can survive change in the *scrambled up world of work* then that's a great life skill. That breadth of experience, lack of fear of failure and love of change at work gives you value in other parts of your life.

I juggle a mix of stuff to keep me happy, stimulated, passionate and the bottom line is so long as we're happy and I'm earning enough money, who cares about anything else?

The spirit of Renaissance Man is at the heart of being a Juggler. Why can't I be a project-manager/micro-entrepreneur/writer/marketing consultant/ideas producer working in loads of client sectors at the same time?

I had a few drinks last night with a bloke I've recently met and we were swapping our stories. He's been a local journalist in Ireland, washed up in Chinese restaurants and managed rock bands. Now he works for a (grown-up) financial institution but with a rich back story. It's who he is and he wouldn't change it for the world. The great thing about being a polymath is not just being talented at loads of different things, it's doing whatever you want united by one criteria: Passion.

Gary Vaynerchuk pulls it off as an entrepreneur, internet celebrity, wine guru, new media commentator, sports fan and video blogger. Who knows what else he's going to add to his portfolio (hey, even Gary doesn't know)? He eschews labels. To some he's 'the wine guy'; to others he is 'the tech guy'. But whatever he's doing, he's mixing it up, he's having fun.

For Gary, it's dead simple: *'My work is my play.'*

For Kevin, it's focusing on what you love: *'Because you only do stuff you love, you tend to be good at the stuff you love.'*

By rethinking work and mastering juggling you can reclaim your life – IT'S ALL ABOUT YOU NOW.

1

Look at success differently

Having it all relies on a fresh way of benchmarking success.

Am I successful? Absolutely, I'd say so.

But if you apply conventional criteria to what I've achieved, some would say I'm not. I'm not a millionaire, I don't own more than one home, and I don't have a stupidly expensive car.

I have a family and two fantastic sons, we have enough money to do most things we want. We usually go away on holiday three times a year. (Mostly) I do what I want, I carve out time to spend with my two young children, I am a published author, I have a rich portfolio of projects and a stimulating work life. I am content, even happy. And I'm very lucky. I try not to forget that.

Success is not just about what you take home in your pay packet but also about being good at what you do, achieving results – and ultimately, it's about having fulfilment. Currency like autonomy, flexibility and making it home for the kids' sports day is just as crucial as the financial kind.

To date I've had a varied career. I've stretched myself in a whole load of new directions, doing things I didn't know I could do, learning all the time.

I've been Managing Director of a small business, managing people, producing a profit and doing all that corporate stuff. Now I run my own one-man business. Largely, I have an enormous amount of choice as to what I do, how I spend my time. The flaw in how popular culture portrays entrepreneurial success is that it is about fast cars and flash-looking offices. And in reality, of course it is not. Who really wants to be a multi-millionaire? Don't we want choice? Isn't that what we all aspire to?

I wouldn't benchmark success on status, job title and number of air miles, I'd rather benchmark it on stuff that really counts: have I had fun? Have I been able to tick off lots of personal ambitions? Have I stretched myself?

And from where it all started – being a teenage radio DJ in Essex and an unpaid extra in a Ray Winstone film – to where I am now – meeting a bunch of people I've always admired and writing my second book – from all I have done in business, I have tried to make a difference. That everyone knew **I was there**. That I helped bring ideas to reality, helped build businesses, delivered projects, whatever. The bottom line is **I'd have it no other**

way – this eclectic mix has made me who I am today.

Juggling is not necessarily about such a wide-ranging portfolio. That's just my own story. What's more important is your story. Ask yourself:

- *!* What do you want to achieve?
- *!* What kind of work life do you want to create?
- *!* How can you ensure you bring your personality to work?
- *!* How can you mix up your passions, work and play?

Use those criteria to measure your success.

So, when we talk of 'having it all' I don't mean sitting on a yacht in the South of France or having a chauffeur-driven limo. It's more grounded than that. It's pulling off a life where you have choice, where you mix personal passions and values with your job, where you are able to sit back and say:

'Life is Good'

(and really mean it).

2

What you do for love and what you do for money

This isn't complicated. When you do what you enjoy, you are instantly happier, because you're having fun. You'll be looking forward to doing the next thing, because you know you'll enjoy it; and then the Work You is not just the Real You but also can be the Best You.

You'll work harder and produce better results, come up with better ideas and perform better. You'll be less stressed, healthier, probably a nicer partner, or even a better parent. And that search for happiness is at the heart of Juggle because it's about carving out a work life based on what you *want*. It's about reclaiming your life.

If you ask entrepreneurs the secret of their success, many will say because they LOVE what they do. After all, how can you be successful if you hate it?

'I certainly can't think what else I'd be doing ... it looks like I'll be juggling for the

foreseeable future. I do love what I do and I don't have the same passion for anything else.'

 *Melanie*

Redesigning your work life means doing some stuff for love and some for money. As we've seen, 20% of what I do probably earns me 80% of my revenue. That means the majority of my meetings and activities don't earn me the most or are even non-billable. Some of that is a business fact of life but it's also symptomatic of where my passions lie: writing books, presenting a bunch of videos. I love that stuff. It doesn't earn me much apart from satisfaction, but remember, a pay packet full of satisfaction is always worth sweating for.

If you aren't stimulated by your current day job, then you need to re-invent it. Try and fall in love with it. If you can't then change something. Add some new stuff to the mix, volunteer to take on more responsibility in pursuit of having more variety and stimulation. Offer to run an after-hours workshop, go on a training course. Write a column for your company magazine or produce a regular departmental newsletter. Consider shifting your working practices. Ask to work flexibly or to work at home sometimes.

There are other ways to mix up what you love with what you need. Actors wait tables in restaurants, illustrators become art teachers, film makers become creative directors, screenplay writers, copywriters. This doesn't dilute their passion. It just gives them a revenue stream and some sense of belonging whilst they continue to pursue their goal. It's being pragmatic; juggling a job and a passion.

Similarly, if you're not intellectually or creatively stretched in your job, consider a hobby or interest to fill that vacuum. So you do karaoke, you DJ, you draw cartoons to round off your business personality.

Freelancers and the self-employed have the freedom to bespoke their Juggle Portfolios with more choice and flexibility. A friend produces corporate videos for straight-laced clients but his real love is film-making and directing. So he juggles stuff he does for love and for money, his business subsidising his passion. Some days he's working for a client, getting paid for it. Other days, he's doing a project which he's funding himself. A work life of just one and not the other would be unsustainable for him. This way – he stays happy.

We all need to re-write our economic models – some things in life you won't get paid for but you'll benefit in other ways. There's loads of value whether it's for motives of altruism or stimulation. You may volunteer or be helping a charity or getting rich life experience.

There are no rules – carve it up!

'I largely get paid to stand in front of people and talk about myself. I do that two or three days a week. The other two or three days a week enable me to do free mentoring for entrepreneurs. I find this really stimulating; there are always new ideas.'

 Mike

3

Create a sustainable economic model and a sustainable lifestyle model

Mixing up passions and diversifying your business interests create sustainability for both the financial viability of your business and your lifestyle.

Mark runs a small business. The company makes radio documentaries, represents clients in music publishing and works as a developer building family homes.

We might expect radio and music to go together, but not radio, music and property. But diversification is good for the bank balance as well as being good for the soul. It's corporate juggling. Mark has succeeded in mixing up his passions, ideas and talents in a business portfolio.

How does he 'get away' with that breadth? Because he is good at what he does, because he has imposed no limits on the business.

He's respected as an all-rounder. His management expertise is a portable skill. An expert in certain areas but also a trusted pair of hands for music and entertainment projects. Diversity doesn't worry his clients, it reassures them. His business can't be a big margin operation making radio documentaries alone, but put it all together and it's a sustainable economic model.

And not just a valid economic model, but also a sustainable lifestyle/enjoyment model. No time for boredom with three balls to juggle, influencing, informing and inspiring the rest.

Before you diversify and take on big new roles, or set up new ventures to juggle, make sure you have stability in one area first.

Melanie Greene has run her Hollywood talent firm for 25 years. She's now embarked on a career as an Executive Producer of film and TV shows at the same time as continuing with the management side. This is a completely different discipline (albeit in the same industry) and takes Melanie away from her core activity, but because of the longevity of her core business, she has the know-how, the staff and the systems and structures to diversify. The other role offers her that diversity, it stimulates her, strengthens her reputation and generates new revenues.

'I always wanted to produce but it took me a while to get to this stage. The management side of the business has always been my bread and butter and I've done very well from it over the years so I've always been careful to make sure that "the base" is secure before engaging in a role because it's very difficult to be a "part time producer". Thankfully, sometimes the two can be compatible.'

 *Melanie*

4

Jugglers have just got to have fun

Try knitting your passions together by punctuating work with play.

When you are a Juggler, you might find there is no boundary between work and play. Because technology allows us to 'work' almost anywhere, many of us start and finish our Juggle Days anywhere but the office. Home. The train. A coffee shop. Wherever. This creates an ease that our parents' generation lacked, but a ton of challenges.

Am I at work or am I at play? Answer: it doesn't bloody matter, so long as you're just being You! Especially when you punctuate the day with snatches of 'play': a work-free zone on a flight to a meeting; a morning's swim; playing tennis in the afternoon. It's invaluable in a long day when you need to stand back from something or just take a breather.

As we've seen, people like Gary have so much fun doing their jobs, they feel like they are at play. Kevin mixes them all together:

'It is all about work, life, play integration. I punctuate constantly. I was up this morning at 6:30, did a couple hours work on stuff that had come in from New York, went down to the gym for an hour session, will then spend some family time and get on to phone calls in Europe. Then 2 hours of tennis, back on to work now that the US is open, a bike ride, a family dinner, and last minute work. It might sound exhausting to some. But every single one of those things was fun for me and a choice.'

 Kevin

I met a young entrepreneur recently who's having so much fun working it just feels like play. When Sam Bompas decided to change his career, he and his school friend Harry set up a company being architectural foodsmiths.* Mixing their love of food and architecture, they make architecture-based jellies – anything from St Paul's Cathedral to a two-metre jelly of Madrid Barajas Airport. His days are a mix of meeting clients, chefs, partners, networking at social events and then hands-on in the kitchen making jellies. On the morning I met Sam he'd been up the night before making jellies. When visitors come to his London house that doubles as the base for the business, they ask 'is it your home

---

*   www.jellymongers.co.uk.

or your office?' Answer – it's both. Jellies have taken over their fridge as their kitchen becomes the base for operations.

The guys are working hard but having loads of fun. From socialising at restaurants with new clients or shopping for fresh fruit and berries at their local Borough Market, Sam feels that 'play and work' are all the same. He's a jelly juggler! And how does he get away with all this? Absolute self belief. Confidence can go a long way in helping you achieve all your juggling dreams.

It's important to have fun. Because whether we sit at a desk or not, we spend a hell of a lot of our lives 'at work' so we might as well enjoy it.

> *'Work and play is all the same to me. It's as much fun for me to stand up in front of a bunch of kids at a school and talk about entrepreneurship as it is to talk to a business audience, as it is to write my column. Everything has to be fun. I don't want to do something I don't enjoy.'*

 Mike

To come up with great ideas, you definitely need time to play around. I got a fax today from Kevin Roberts, with one of his trademark handwritten notes on an email I'd sent him:

'I'm in Cannes this week, staying at my St Tropez home, playing tennis, cycling, running the network, living Juggle and lovin' it.'

 Kevin

And it doesn't get better than that!

5

You don't need to be the boss to have it all

Don't think that 'Having It All' is an option only for people like Gary Vaynerchuk and Kevin Roberts, or people running their own businesses. It's for all of us.

A guy I know is a copywriter working in-house at a big technology company. He loves to write. The press releases and brochures he writes in his day job don't always give him 100% satisfaction but his real love is creative writing; he writes screenplays and novels. And the 'down time' in his day job gives him the mental space to think about his personal projects. He's not taking the p**s, he's delivering on all fronts for the job but working in a culture where he can find mental space throughout the day. His employers are flexible about the hours he works, so he can disappear to the gym late morning or early afternoon and he can leave the office early enough help with his kids' bath time and read them a story. And he still carves out an hour or so a day to sit down and work on his screenplay. He's not going to stay in the job forever but right now it suits him. It gives him financial stability and the freedom to juggle with his passions and his lifestyle. 'It's a pretty good gig,' he said to me, and he's right. Sometimes success is just being true to your goals and 'getting away' with what you want out of life.

Dave is another example of a Juggler. His passion is photography. But he does other stuff too, because he wants to, and because he needs to pay the bills. Dave works at a camera store, he runs art shows, he goes into local schools and teaches photography to kids, he's a commercial photographer for hire. Some of which he does for love, others for money. He even helps out his brother-in-law, labouring.

He might not have traditional career status but he's happy and he's doing his own thing. He's doing what he loves; he's carved out what he wants to do.

He's living The Juggle Life.

6

Living life version 3.4

If you are going to 'have it all', you need to be comfortable with uncertainty. You need to be able to revel in a '*I have no idea precisely where this is going*' culture because, when you choose the Juggle life, you need to acknowledge things may still be a work in progress, constantly being polished and reviewed to improve and enhance.

Having it all is about chucking away the rule book and being open to experimentation and new possibilities. That means forget the Five Year personal or business plan. Think five months into the future, not five years. We cannot predict the future. That can be scary or unsettling. How long am I in this job for? What happens if the recession hits my industry? What happens if I decide to relocate to a new city? What's most important in living your life is that flexibility, not some carefully crafted rigid life plan. It's what life coach and blogger Melissa Pierce has billed, **'Life In Perpetual Beta'.***

---

*　www.lifeinperpetualbeta.com.

Our lives are a work-in-progress. That uncertainty means sometimes you have to wait. It might take a while for something to come to fruition, so recognise that when you are juggling multiple goals, some you'll score quickly but others might have to wait. And to keep them all in the air you need to make sure you're not too short-sighted or that you get frustrated and want to ditch projects before they have realised their potential.

And ultimately, when life is in perpetual beta, you need to be realistic. Some days are going to better than others. Some days you'll have to do projects or tasks you don't fancy but that's the *quid pro quo* for all the benefits you enjoy.

> *'It's a bit like when I was in a band. You do a fifty date tour and some gigs are better than others. For some reason at some it hasn't happened, it wasn't that great and then the next gig is stellar, and my life is very much like that.'*

 Mike

7

Having freedom of choice

I was driving back home on the motorway listening to the radio. There was a phone-in: listeners were calling in to answer the question, 'What would you do if you could do anything tomorrow?' People phoned in, their voices brimming with enthusiasm and passion for doing 'anything but the 9–5'. Their passion shone through. One woman said she would go horse riding; another would turn her hobby into a new business. But they were all slaves to the 9–5, and these were destined to remain dreams. Not one of them could actually do what they dreamt of.

But as I continued the drive home I had a real buzz. I didn't *have* to go to an office the next day, I could work at home. I literally had real choices on what I would do the next day. If I really wanted to, I could take the day off.

Some of that freedom is because I am my own boss, but it's also about carving out a role doing what I enjoy and what I am good at. Juggle is about making choices. What do YOU want to do, how do YOU want to do it? I'm not a slave to something I hate, I focus on only doing what I'm passionate about.

The truth is that people strive to do what they love rather than earn loads of money. Workers want MEANING in their life. They want fulfilment. Choice is often under-rated as a lifestyle commodity. Yet it's what all of us crave, rather than a big pay packet.

Jan is an HR Manager who decided to become a Juggler, to mix it all up, to be empowered with choice. She's carved out a role as HR manager three days per week and jewellery designer and arts festival organiser the rest of her time. Cut her down the middle and you won't find HR policy and procedure: you'll find creativity and passion in her DNA. And that's what drives her. If she wants to do Pilates at 3pm on a Friday she can. She's had enough of doing it other people's way, she's doing it her way. She's become a Juggler.

From mixing up HR and the arts, to mixing up projects and expansion for a global brand, Jugglers can live their dream lives.

8

RETIRE RETIREMENT

We're told that the trend for more people working past their retirement age is due to people living longer and their falling pension provision. But one reason a lot of people in their 60s and 70s are working is simple: they enjoy it; without it they'd be bored. After all, there is only so much playing golf and redecorating the house that can be done.

Yes – people are **choosing** to carry on working (crazy, huh?!).

It's hardly a surprise, is it? So if you love what you do, why retire?

I heard of an entrepreneur who retired to Thailand. But he soon got bored sailing and playing golf so decided to develop a new project instead. He couldn't turn off his work persona, it's who he is. And so long as you take time to enjoy life, there's nothing wrong with that.

A friend of mine in her 50s who has carved out a whole new (and successful) working life certainly has no intentions of retiring in the traditional sense of moving to a bungalow or going on a cruise holiday. As she said to me, 'Why on earth would I want to be herded onto a cruise ship?!' She's leading a fuller and more satisfying life than ever. Relocating, entering a new phase in her life and 'taking it easy' is not on her agenda. And she wouldn't change it for the world; I'm with her 100%.

The notion of retirement that you go one day from working full time to the next day totally free is flawed anyway. You can still be economically active in your later years but have more choice of how, where and when you work. Actually, that shouldn't only be a mantra for your retirement, apply that across your life now.

Work is good for the soul, and if you're going to have a 50-year+ career rather than 40 years, juggling is more important than you think, so find time for your passions NOW, before it's too late. Don't stick in a job you hate in pursuit of a goal of economic freedom at retirement. What's the point? Start living your dreams now, carve out a life of work and play driven by what you enjoy and do it until you want to stop.

When I was in my early 30s a few friends used to talk of their retirement goals: to be 'on the golf course' by the time they were 50, to have enough revenue streams so as not to work.

So the traditional retirement model went like this: work flat out from 9 in the morning to 6 at night, while you are aged 20–50. Earn stacks of money. Jeopardise relationships with family. Don't see your kids grow up. Stop when you are 50 or 55 and start gardening or golf.

Bollocks!

How about this as an alternative Juggle Manifesto?

Work hard but flexibly. Mix up work and play so you see your kids while you're still young, see them growing up. Live for the moment. Find time for your passions. Take plenty of holidays. Work until you want to stop, no retirement. Sure, include holidays and taking it easy, but mix up business, social, leisure, travel interests.

Which option do you prefer?

Whatever your retirement goals, start incorporating them into your life now.

9

The work you = the real you

It's a great feeling when your job or business is an extension of you, your personality and philosophies; where all are intertwined.

All of our Jugglers have pulled that off and there's plenty more examples I see every day. Richard René runs a business consultancy based in Idaho; his offering is centred on his love of networking and connecting different people. That's what he says he is as a human being; and that's his business. His website displays a 'personal note' communicating his personal *raison d'être* at the heart of his business offering:

'My business is a reflection and extension of my inherently social and inquisitive nature. The networking I have done around the globe has an obvious commercial value and has seasoned and spiced my life with a diverse collection of long and strong friendships. Both my personal and professional lives contribute to my hunger for perspectives on life from all over the world. From current events, to family, and cultural riches, getting to know people around the world and becoming familiar with their perspectives on all kinds of topics, contributes enormously to both the intellect and the spirit – with my only rule to remain as open as possible to all perspectives.'

Richard René*

And lots of us run our lives like that. Our life partners are our business partners; chat around the dinner party table is about our work and business lives. Clients become friends, friends become clients as the Real You and the Work You become intertwined.

---

* www.reneglobal.com.

Whilst Richard's juggling mixes his love of networking, for one guy I met recently it's about mixing behind a bar. Ian Burrell started working behind a bar when he left school and hasn't looked back – he's integrated his own passions into his work life.

Ian's #1 passion is rum. Billed as the UK's Rum Ambassador, he runs *Rumfest*, travels the world working with rum brands, has a Caribbean restaurant in North London and is planning the launch of a new tapas bar. The restaurant could easily be a full-time role in itself so Ian is careful to segment his time well and delegate to a good team who look after the restaurant. But Ian likes to stay hands-on when he can, he loves working behind a bar, that's his 'stage' and his true passion so he still makes time for that at the same time as running the business.

To Ian, this doesn't feel like a job – he's doing what he loves and getting paid for it. When he wakes up in the morning he can't wait to get started to conquer the to-do list and emails. But whatever he does in his life, the bar – and that passion for rum – is the constant theme throughout his life.

A couple of stories from Jugglers prove what's possible when you wrap up your lifestyle in your work brand – you can have it all.

10

Are you a lifeaholic?

I try to avoid being a workaholic, but am happy to be a lifeaholic. That means I'm passionate about life and work. I don't just live for the weekends and holidays, I enjoy work. Sometimes that means doing some work seven days a week. But I also try to have some 'play' every day too, whether a run, being back for the kids' bathtime, having a laugh, whatever. Being a Lifeaholic is not about seeking a work/life balance; it's maximising all parts of your life.

Being a lifeaholic is being as close as possible to your 'ideal' life: if I can pull all that off, then that's a result. I read about a designer who moved out of the city to the country so her children could have a great quality of life. She recognises that for a few nights a week she needs to be away from them in London for business, but the rest of time she works at home and spends time with the children. The countryside bit inspires her, the city stimulates her; she's juggling.

I feel lucky. Apart from some inevitable tweaking, the shape of my life is pretty much what I want. Sure, more holidays, a second home in the South of France, a retainer with a big client, some more revenues might make a difference but generally I'm in a good place. And that feels good.

Having it all as a Juggler is about seeking your ideal work life, but also being realistic on what is achievable; so you might need some reality checks along the way (if your dream is dating Beyoncé Knowles and living on Necker Island, move on).

But if your dream is realistic, go for it. Start living it now.

11

Ticking your boxes

Having it all is reaching a stage in life when you can start ticking the boxes of how you live your life, and fulfilling your passions and desires. Whether you are Kevin the CEO or Dave the Photographer it's about your life reflecting your passions.

It's also moulding your work life to suit your own needs. A woman I know is relocating from Europe to the States but shaping her work life around criteria from her personal wish list; the summer will see her based back in the company's European offices so her family can spend time with relatives back there. She's seeking 'the best of both worlds'.

Another executive fed up with decades of commuting three hours a day wanted a radical change. He moved countries and swapped the commute he hated for a 30-minute journey with a fantastic quality of life. He wrote into his personal plan to return to the UK at least four times a year to see his family. More boxes ticked.

I read about a guy who quit his job in the city to go and work in the Caribbean. He realised that nowhere else would he be able to go and swim in the ocean before work and have a climate that better suited him. He still works hard but in a different way; it's a very different kind of pressure. Life is all-consuming. Frenetic, busy, 24/7 but with one important difference. He's doing what he loves.

But you don't have to go to the Caribbean to live your dream life. You can make small changes to your job that can make a big difference. A former colleague has recently joined a new company and is benefitting from an improvement in his quality of life. The company culture has work hours of 10 to 6 which means he can have a more leisurely start in the morning. By getting a scooter he has also reduced his commute to the office from an unpredictable tube journey of nearly an hour to a 15-minute ride. Two small things that have brought him significant change.

When you're looking to tick your boxes, try setting goals on where you want to go, then track your progress. I set myself goals at the beginning of each year, and (remarkably) I meet most of them. For example, on 4 January 2007 I articulated a goal in my notepad, that the book idea I was then working on would come to fruition, get published and be on the shelves in Borders. Twelve months later that dream came to reality – my first book was published and there it was on the shelves in the bookstore. I believed in the goal, I believed in its ability to come off, therefore it happened.

You'll also need self-belief and the confidence to realise those dreams. I watched some of the interviews with the medal winners at the 2008 Beijing Olympics. So many said they had visualised winning Gold, they had believed they could achieve it. And that vision is immensely powerful.

Without dreams and vision like that you may not extend yourself to your full potential. Have ambition and endeavour to get those boxes ticked.

12

Have you worked out what's really important?

The great thing about living the Juggle Life is having that sense of purpose of knowing what's important in life and what's not important.

It's following Kevin's mantra of 'playing where you play well' and forgetting the rest. You can feel liberated by focusing on your passions and values not just in your work life but through everything. That clarity is such a great tool for navigating life: I know what's important and, similarly, I know what I'm not going to waste my time doing. Amen to that.

Whatever is in those boxes to tick, creating a Juggle life relies on listening to your heart. That may sound cheesy but it's recognising the important stuff such as health and quality of life rather than material status or wealth.

Chris is a Juggler; he runs a group of boutique businesses in publishing, design and animation. His business operations wrap up his passions: he loves seeing his ideas come to fruition. He's put in place teams and systems to manage the businesses day-to-day and he dips in to troubleshoot, lead a project or negotiate with a client or new recruit. It's taken a lot of sweat to get the business to this stage but it works. Two days a week Chris works at the company offices in Central London, the rest of the week he works from home.

When his wife was diagnosed with cancer, he'd just got the business to a stage where it could be more self-sufficient, so he was able to step back to help his wife through surgery whilst the business did its own thing. Chris and his wife always had the goal of spending the winter months in Australia or the Caribbean, running their respective businesses from there and coming back to London for the summer. That goal was three years away but, following the discovery of cancer, they've decided to bring that forward.* It's about focusing on quality of life and health as priorities, integrated with the business needs.

It's about reviewing and realigning goals to reflect what really counts through all your life. Putting work into perspective and knowing what the real priorities are.

---

*   The surgery went well and his wife is now in recovery.

13

Live in the now and fulfil your dreams

A piece of advice:

Try to live in the now, in the moment.
Don't delay your dreams, aspirations or passions.
Don't say you'll wait five years or 20 years until your exit or retirement plan. Don't put your dreams on hold.

Because we never know what's round the corner.

We often hear stories of people who had great plans for the future but their ideas had to remain dreams because of poor health or a change in circumstances. So have the courage to listen to your heart.

Don't say to yourself you'll 'work like a dog' for five more years and then start juggling; or **then** start incorporating your passions or flexibility, or **then** start spending time with your family.

Don't think 'then'; **do 'now'.**

Juggling effectively means you can integrate your hopes, dreams and passions now, not at some stage in the future. And without making unnecessary sacrifices.

If you're not convinced of the importance of having dreams and trying to achieve them, watch Randy Pausch's *Last Lecture**. Randy Pausch was an academic and scientist who died in July 2008 after pancreatic cancer. The *Last Lecture* series at Carnegie Mellon University was designed to let academics give a lecture to students – imagining it was their last – to leave them with an important message. This took on huge significance when Randy Pausch gave his lecture in September 2007 with the knowledge that he had been given only months to live. In the lecture he talks about how important it is to '*have fun today, tomorrow and every other day I have*'. Randy had many childhood dreams; most of which he fulfilled, including being an 'Imagineer' at Disney. Through his work and teaching he also helped inspire other people to achieve their dreams.

So have a dream and aim to fulfil it. Like all of us, I had a bunch of childhood dreams. Some were destined to always remain dreams (I never did date Cheryl Ladd from *Charlie's Angels*!) but others I fulfilled. To present a radio show. To meet and interview some of my idols. And then as I grew up, more goals. To work in television. To work in the music industry. To be on the board

---

* www.thelastlecture.com.

of a company, to start my own small business, to become a father, to have a book published. And I have ticked those. But you have to keep dreaming and you have to keep progressing.

Randy Pausch's mantra was that 'we cannot change the cards we are dealt, just how we play the hand'.

So go for it now. Incorporate your wishes into your daily life.

And when things are getting on top of you; when you are feeling really stressed, remember to put things in perspective.

> *'Whenever I get too extreme my husband always reminds me of Billy Connolly's line: No-one ever has on their tombstone "I wish I'd spent more time at the office!"'*

 *Melanie*

14

The bottom line = leave a legacy

Living the juggling life is not just being passionate about what you do. It's making a difference, putting meaning into life. It's valuing your contribution.

So answer this: what IS your *raison d'etre*? What do *you* want to contribute to Planet Earth?

Kevin tries to focus on stuff that makes a difference; his driving belief is to '*make the world a better place for everyone*'.

So make sure your juggling is not without meaning. Here's Mike's:

> **'You have to have a good set of principles in the way you do business. When I talk about how to run business ethically I always talk about telling the truth, treat people in business the way you want to be treated, and if you can help people without detriment to your business... the more you put into the world it comes back again.'**

 Mike

THINK: What do you want your epitaph to be?

That's the bottom line.

Here's what I would like mine to be:

! Ian Sanders made a difference.

! He did what he wanted.

! He enjoyed a good quality of life.

! He did things differently.

! He didn't waste time. If he wanted to do something, he did it.

What's yours?

15

It's make your mind up time

Living the Juggle Life means you can rethink and challenge the old assumptions about work and business; you can mix up work and play; you can fulfil your dreams in order to have it all.

You need to make a choice.

In the Old Economy we worked for 40 years, burned ourselves out and retired. Juggling has changed all that, opening whole new doors of opportunity. Now, we mix it up, we live as we go along and do whatever we want to do.

In this world, there is no right or wrong; you can live your story your way and stick to it. Those who eschew traditional career progression are the ones who have it all. They are the ones with the interesting stories.

Living the Juggle Life is about being honest, being authentic about who you really are and having a sense of purpose.

So at the end of the day you have a choice.

You can play it the old way. Work your way up the career ladder, follow traditional career development, be a slave to the organisation, work for a straight financial return. And then retire.

Or you can take the Juggle route.

Live by your passions, focus on what you're good at and what you love doing (don't worry about all the other stuff). Go beyond the job title, avoid being pigeonholed, and have lots of strings to your bow, mix up work and play and celebrate being multi-dimensional. Strive to be not just the *Real You*, but also the *Best You* and the *Happiest You*.

You decide. ...

> *'Jugglers rule! We're the ones that will find fulfilment. Francis Ford Coppola told me a couple of months back when we were speaking together in Buenos Aires that no matter what we're all doing now, he knows how the story ends. We all die. The trick is that some people live a life, and leave a legacy. Many don't. Jugglers do.'*

 Kevin

Happy Juggling. ...

THE JUGGLER'S MANIFESTO

Success in Juggling is about having the right spirit. It's having a whole toolbox of the right mindset to deal with everything that gets thrown at you. So here's the Juggler's Manifesto:

1 FORGET SPECIALISM, discover the value of being across more than one discipline. Sticking to just one thing limits your potential; place no limits on what you do and become more fulfilled.

2 BE PASSIONATE about all you do; let your passions and desires inform and shape your work life.

3 BE ADEPT AT GEAR-SHIFTING, from segueing from the huge to the tiny, from work to play.

4 MAKE TIME FOR PLAY. Being a successful Juggler is about working hard but also mixing up work and play, and using playtime as your inspiration and stimulation.

5 BE A CHAMELEON, FLEXIBLE AND ADAPTABLE. Rethink all you do, be happy to change the rules again and again. Don't stay entrenched in rigid ideas of how things should be done.

6 THE BEST PLAN IS A NON-PLAN. Success in the knowledge economy is about making it up as you go along.

7 USE YOUR INSTINCT (every time) in making decisions, in deciding what to do and what not to do.

8 RE-DEFINE PERSONAL SUCCESS not by a salary package alone but by more important currency such as, did you get to see your kid's sports day, do you work with a decent bunch of people, did you take enough holiday this year?

9 GO BEYOND A JOB TITLE and carve out a unique You-role. Do it your way, be authentic. Take control.

10 DEVELOP A PERSONAL BRAND to unite and communicate your strengths.

11 WORK HARD BUT WORK *SMART*. Whilst success relies on you working hard it's also about doing what you love; and when you do what you love, it doesn't feel so much like work.

12 HAVE LOTS OF SELF-BELIEF AND SELF-CONFIDENCE. Have a positive outlook, be an optimist. Don't whinge!

13   BE A PIONEER, with no fear of the unknown. Be happy to learn new stuff, embrace new ideas.

14   HAVE PURPOSE IN ALL YOU DO. Focus on making a difference and leaving a legacy.

Index

accidental success 66–8, 191
attitude
    to starting a new business 17
    and success 4, 38
authenticity 61–3, 191
autonomy 53–4

Balazs, André 20
Beach Walks TV vii, 95, 102, 143–4
Bird, Andy 66–7
BlackBerry 86
Blair, Tony 57
blogging 45, 92, 101–3, 116, 143–4, 146–7
blurring, life and work 44–6
branding *see* personal branding
Burrell, Ian 176

career
    breaks 47–8
    development 26, 27
chameleon 100, 112, 190
change 1–2, 7–8
    re-invention 1, 55–6, 158
choice 24, 42–3, 53, 155, 187–9
    freedom of 170–1
    and retirement 172–4
coffee shops 121
comfort zone 63–4

communication, filtering 110–11
confidence 4, 40, 61, 165, 180, 191
connections
    networking 91–3, 101, 175
    technology 86–8
core competencies/roles 64, 162
corporate juggling 46–8, 53–4
courage 4, 34, 40, 64, 183

Darling, Roxanne vii–viii
    juggle tactics 82, 87–8, 92, 95–6, 102, 106, 134, 143–4
    life redesign 64–5, 67
    rethinking work 13–14
deadlines 80–1
delegation 138–41
deletion tactics 106–8
detail, importance of 105–6
development 149
    career development 26, 27
diversity 161–2
    connections and 91–2
    of places 122
    quirkiness and 117–18
dream fulfillment 183–5

economic model, sustainable 160–2
ecosystem, personal 119–21
80/20 rule 98, 158

emails 74, 86, 110–11, 142
entrepreneurs
    importance of familiy to 31,
        119–20
    working for love 157–8
entry barriers 16
exercise 59–60, 129, 133–5
experimentation 63–5

Facebook 44–5, 101
family 144–6
    guilt and 143
    time with 86–7
    and work 29–31, 119–20
fitness 133–5
flexibility 3, 74, 168, 190
    flexible working 18–19, 21–2,
        33, 34, 167
focus 11, 73, 84–5, 146
freedom of choice 170–1
fun 67, 157, 163–6, 184

gear shifting 57–8, 190
generalisation 13–16
    commercial value of 52
    versus specialism 11–13, 190
    see also plurality
Generation Y 32–3
goal setting 39–41, 180, 182
Google 46, 141
Greene, Melanie vi–vii
    juggle lifestyle 161–2
    juggle tactics 83, 95, 129,
        134–5, 139–40
guidelines, set of 120
guilt 143–4

hands-on approach 65–6
having it all 166–7
    best of both worlds 178–80
health 40, 89, 129, 181, 182
high-maintenance relationships 94

hobby businesses 16–17, 61
home
    life 144–6
    working from 18–19, 45
hours worked 21–3

ideas generation 124–5, 132
identity management 114–16
information
    deletion of 106–8
    filtering 110–11
    flow of 141–2
Innocent Drinks 46
inspiration jaunt 123–6
instinct 67, 68, 107–8, 191

James, Sid 62
jellies 164–5
job
    learning on the 63–5
    for life 25–7
    sharing 34
    title 26, 27–9, 191
Johnson, Luke 31
journalism 69

Last Lecture (Pausch) 184, 185
Law, Andy 46–7
learning on the job 63–5
legacy, leaving a 186–7, 192
life coaching 39, 69
life redesign 37–8
    'accidental success' 66–8, 191
    authenticity 61–3, 191
    autonomy in 53–4
    corporate juggling 46–8, 53–4
    gear shifting 57–8, 190
    learning on the job 63–5
    and multi-dimensional
        talents 48–50, 114–16,
        117–18
    multi-tasking 69–70, 152

options and choices 42–3
playtime 59–60, 129, 163–6,
    190
re-invention 1, 55–6, 158
the real you 51–2
setting goals 39–41
staying hands-on 65–6
stimulation and 136
work/life blur in 44–6
lifeaholics 177–8
lifestyle 151–3
    best of both worlds 178–80
    deciding on 187–9
    freedom of choice 170–1
    having fun 163–6
    having it all 166–7, 178–80
    leaving a legacy 186–7, 192
    lifeaholic 177–8
    living in the now 183–5
    love and money 157–60
    priorities 181–2
    retirement and 172–4
    success and 154–6, 191
    sustainable 160–2
    uncertainty and 168–9
    work you/real you 174–6
Linked In 101
list making 78–9, 82
living in the now 183–5
love, working for 157–60
low-maintenance
        relationships 93–4

maintenance 148
manifesto, juggler's 190–2
Mason Zimbler 3
'me' time 87
meetings 108–10
mini breaks 123–6
money 24–5, 158–60
    sustainability and 160–2
Mother (ad agency) 115

motivation 135–6
multi-dimensional talents 48–50,
        114–16, 117–18
multi-tasking 69–70, 152

networking 91–3, 101, 175
    support network 137–8
non-plan 66–8, 191

office work 18–20
one-man branding 101–3
Outlook 141, 142
outsourcing 138–41

panic, dealing with 89–91
passion 4, 11, 61, 140, 152,
        157–60, 190
Pausch, Randy 184, 185
perfectionism 85
perpetual beta 168–9
personal assistants 111, 137–8
    virtual 111, 136, 141–2
personal branding 99–100, 191
    identity management 114–16
    one-man branding 101–3
    and quirkiness 116–18
    work you/real you 174–6
personal computing *see* technology
personal script 111–13
personalisation 62
Peters, Tom 37
pigeon-holing 27, 28, 49
    see also specialism
places, different 121–2
playtime 59–60, 129, 163–6, 190
plurality 2–4
    and multi-dimensional
        talents 48–50, 114–16,
        117–18
    and success 8–10
    see also generalisation
podcasts 95, 102, 107, 141, 143–4

portfolio workers 40, 51–2, 57,
       159, 160–1
power 25, 42, 53
Prior, David 14–15
prioritisation 81–4, 97, 146–7
    and lifestyle 181–2
productivity 21–3
project making 80–1
purpose, sense of 181, 186–7, 192

quality of life 32, 54, 128, 177, 179
quirkiness 116–18

rationing, time 74
re-invention 1, 55–6, 158
recession proofing 8, 43, 50
relationships
    building effective 93–6
    networking 91–3, 101, 175
Renaissance Man 12, 152
René, Richard 175
results 19, 21, 22
retirement 172–4
rewards 126–8
Roberts, Kevin vi
    juggle tactics 87, 92, 114,
       120–2, 125, 133–4, 137–41
    life redesign 38, 47–8
    rethinking work 6, 12–13
ROWE (results-only-work-
    environment) 22
rule book 16–17
rum 176

Saatchi & Saatchi vi, 47, 114,
       137–8
sabbaticals 47–8
St Luke's 46–7
scheduling 74–5
segmentation 76–7
self-belief 40, 165, 180, 191
self employment 34–5, 159, 160–1

self-immersion 105–6
selling yourself 99–100
seven year itch 56
'slack time' 46
sleep 134
Sloly, David 3
social life 145
Southon, Mike vii
    juggle lifestyle 186
    juggle tactics 86–7, 102, 110–
       12, 117–18, 133
    life redesign 55–6, 60–2, 68
    rethinking work 15
specialism
    versus generalisation 11–13, 190
    a job for life 25
    see also pigeon-holing
Spinvox 111
status quo 34–6
stimulation 135–6
stress busting 88–91
success
    accidental 66–8, 191
    attitude and juggling skills 4, 38
    and lifestyle 154–6, 191
    money and 24
    and plurality 8–10
support network 137–8
survival 7
sustainability 160–2

tactics, juggling 71–2
    coming up for air 131–2
    connections 91–3
    delegation and
       outsourcing 138–41
    deletion 106–8
    filtering information 110–11
    fitness and 133–5
    focusing 84–5, 146
    get unplugged 86–8
    guilt and 143–4

home life and 144–6
identity management 114–16
inspiration jaunt 123–6
list making 78–9, 82
meetings 108–10
one-man branding 101–3
personal ecosystem 119–21
personal script 111–13
places and 121–2
prioritisation 81–4, 97, 146–7
project making 80–1
quirkiness and 116–18
relationship building 93–6
segmentation 76–7
self-immersion 105–6
sell yourself 99–100
and stimulation 135–6
stress busting 88–91
support network 137–8
thinking ahead 148–9
time management 73–5,
    146–8
treating yourself 126–8
and the unexpected 103–5
value criteria 96–8
virtual assistants 111, 136,
    141–2
workaholism, avoiding
    128–30
talent 4, 21
multi-dimensional 48–50,
    114–16, 117–18
tangibles, focus on 84
teams, as support 137–8
technology 44–5
and branding 101–3
deletion tactics 106–8
and life redesign 44–5
and personal identity 115–16
and rethinking work 7, 14–15,
    16–17
screening 111

unplugging 86–8
    see also blogging; emails;
        podcasts; virtual work
thinking ahead 148–9
3M 46
time management 73–5, 146–8
time out 123–6
to-do lists 82
translators 13–14
treats 126–8
triage 79, 81–2
Twitter 45, 92, 101

uncertainty 168–9
unexpected, preparation for
    103–5
unplugging, connections 86–8

value criteria 96–8
variety, benefits of 43
Vaynerchuk, Gary v
    juggle tactics 102–3, 110, 113,
        153
    life redesign 42, 49
    rethinking work 10
video podcasts v, 102, 143–4
virtual work 6, 18
    assistants 111, 136, 141–2
voicemails 110–11

Walt Disney International 66–7
Wine Library TV v, 102
Wired magazine 147
work
    blurring with life 44–6
    hard and smart 38, 191
    and play 59–60, 129, 163–6,
        190
work, rethinking 1–2, 6
    change and 7–8
    family and 29–31, 119–20
    generalisation and 13–16

a job for life 25–7
job title 26, 27–9, 191
money and 24–5, 158–60
office work 18–20
plurality and 2–4, 8–10
productivity 21–3
and the rule book 16–17

specialism and 11–13, 190
status quo and 34–6
work/life balance 32–3, 38
workaholics 35, 128–30
working from home 18–19, 45

yoga 134–5